YOUR BELIEFS ARE THE REASONS WHY

PATTY! SHEA

Library of Congress Control Number: 2021917859

ISBN Hardcover 978-1-0879-0546-4
ISBN eBook 978-1-0879-0594-5
ISBN Paperback 978-1-0879-7887-1

Printed in the United States of America.

The intent of the author is only to offer information of a general nature in your quest for emotional and spiritual well-being. In the event you use any of the information in this book for yourself, the author and the publisher assume no responsibility for your actions.

Author Disclaimer: I have tried to recreate events, locales and conversations from my memories of them. In order to maintain their anonymity in some instances I have changed the names of individuals and places, I may have changed some identifying characteristics and details such as physical properties, occupations and places of residence.

Inspired by those who helped shape my life lessons.
Dedicated to those who dream of something more.

'Know your passion is lifting up others! Patty!

CONTENTS

INTRODUCTION

What the hell? I was responsible for not making Vice President of Operations and it was not the current Operations Vice President holding me back? And I find this out with only nine months before I retire and after thirty-nine years with the same company, trying to get there? Really? How did this happen? Was there something I could have done differently? How much of my fate was in my control?

This realization came near the end of that long career. A wise and dear friend sweetly asked, "Do you want to know more about this?"

"No!" I retorted. I did not realize working through the answer to this question would have such a profound impact on my life going forward. I would learn that our thoughts, feelings and beliefs are key to whatever we want.

That wonderful friend, Michele, waited for another time when I was in that wished-it-would-have-turned-out-differently mood to pose the question again. "Patty, do you want to know more about this?"

Exhausted, this time I replied, "Yes."

She then hit me with this one powerful question, "What if your *belief* the VP was holding you back was what was actually holding you back from reaching your goal?" I was dumbstruck, and as the old saying goes, it hit me like a ton of bricks. I got that feeling in the pit of my stomach similar to when something resonates because there must be some truth to it. Dang!

I do not remember all the specifics of what she said after that. I just remember her question lingering in my mind. It permeated my whole being. I felt sad and disappointed in myself. How could I have been so deaf to my own thoughts, to my Patty-created beliefs? I let one misguided thought limit me from accomplishing the only goal I had not achieved in my career: Vice President of Operations of our local electric and natural gas utility.

My story is just that, my story. You have your story. No matter where you are in your personal, emotional, spiritual or physical journey, I hope my words and story tug softly at your heart and your inner self, calling you to explore. My hope is you take some time to question those things unattained. I hope you ponder, *What were my thoughts? What did I feel and come to believe as fact? How did it influence my life? More importantly, what do I choose to think, feel and believe from now on?* Your beliefs are the reasons why.

CHAPTER 1
IT STARTED IN THE GARDEN

How did I reach this place in my professional life after thirty-nine years with the same company? Why was this my belief all those years? What had I thought, felt and then believed that brought me to this shocking realization?

It started when I was very young. It started in the garden. Before school-age, probably at age four or five, I remember picking weeds in the garden with my mom, dad, older brother and both of my older sisters. There were four of us kids, and I proudly acknowledge I was the spoiled baby! Donna was the oldest, followed by Tom (Tommy), Jan (Jannie) and then me. Mom and Dad, but more often Mom, instilled in us that we needed to be good, honest, respectful and humble human beings. That was my memory, my perception.

Consequently, during the summer months of elementary school (it was commonly called grade school back then), we were responsible for additional chores than during the school year, like weeding the garden and flower beds. My daily chores throughout the year were making my bed, of course, emptying the garbage from all rooms and cleaning the bathroom. These are the ones I remember.

Of all the additional summer chores, picking weeds was the one I loathed. We had flower beds, tree and shrub beds and a vegetable garden. There were always so many weeds. Summer also brings back the smell of freshly mown grass and the sound of bed sheets flapping in the wind on Dad's homemade clothesline. I can almost smell the freshness of those stiff cotton sheets and remember the rough feel of the wind-dried bath towels as we unpinned them from the clothesline and placed them in the white, wire rectangle clothes basket. This basket served a dual purpose as a picnic basket when we would head to Lake Coeur d'Alene, a forty-minute drive from Spokane, Washington, east to Coeur d'Alene, Idaho. In the early '60s, we went to watch the annual hydroplane races.

Summer memories also bring back the faint smell of Oly (Olympia) beer. Sometimes on those very hot, dry summer days, Dad would sip on one can of Oly or Black Label beer. Money had been tight for Dad growing up in a small Minnesota town, and it was the same for us growing up going to a private grade school in Spokane. Dad had witnessed what too much beer could do to a person, relationships and families. As a result, he did not buy much beer and rarely bought liquor. When he did buy beer, it was the cheaper Oly (Olympia Brewing Company, Tumwater, Washington) and Black Label (Carling Brewing Company, Canada).

Dad's folks, Grandpa and Grandma Shea, lived at the end of our block three homes away by way of a bumpy, dirt alley. Dad would encourage me to spend time with my grandpa. To this little girl, Grandpa seemed very old and kind of scary, probably because he was not much for conversation. An easy way for me to spend time with him was to accompany Dad when he would head to Grandpa's and Grandma's with that Oly in hand, on a hot afternoon after he mowed the lawn. Once Dad let me have a little sip of that bitter-tasting liquid refreshment. I disliked it then and still am not a beer fan. I remember inquiring with distain, "Why do you drink sour water?"

His response: "It quenches my thirst."

Grandpa Shea had a fabric bench swing, with a canvas awning, perched by the side of his garage on the attached patio. Dad and I would walk down the dusty alley together. Grandpa would be expecting us. He would be seated at one end of the swing, Dad would sit at the other end. Being pretty young, I had to jump up on it in order to sit between them. I can still feel the awkwardness of the three of us, swinging mostly in silence, except for the sound of the squeaky bench springs. Neither Dad nor Grandpa cared for nor felt comfortable with lots of chatter, especially their own. But the memory is strong: exchanging our hellos, me jumping on the swing while Dad held it from moving, my little legs sticking straight out, as they were not long enough to bend over the edge of cushion. There we would be swinging, the hot, dry air feeling a little cooler as we swayed back and forth, with Dad sipping his beer, and no one saying anything.

I believe my four-year old self still lies quietly, deep down in my psyche. I have a strong sense of duty and responsibility and a need to do the right thing, in all instances. It is important to me to make others feel valued. I love to make others laugh and find the humor in daily life, using me and my antics as the fodder for their laughter. My heart hurts for the down-trodden and for those who have a life of struggle and sorrow. Many times I feel guilty for the simple luxuries life has afforded me. I cry at the simplest things, especially heart-tugging television commercials involving puppies and kids. I cannot watch ads for the American Society for the Prevention of Cruelty to Animals (ASPCA). When I even hear the music start to play as the commercial comes on, I have to turn off the sound and immediately change the channel. Of course I love the Hallmark channel and usually have tissues handy to watch a holiday marathon of love finds a way. These things still influence who I am.

I remember a hot, summer day in the garden in the late morning, the six of us picking weeds. I was being very careful not to pick an immature carrot, radish, pea or bean. Tommy (the loving nickname we three girls have for our brother, Tom) who is seven years older than me, took off his shirt to cool himself. As I watched, I remember thinking, "I'm hot, too!" So I proceeded to pull my short-sleeve shirt, probably a hand-me-down from Tommy, over my head.

This is my first recollection that some things were not going to be fair in my life, in my little-girl opinion. It was perfectly fine he took his shirt off, but taking mine off, oh my gosh! My mom about flipped. "Patty, put your shirt back on!" Mom demanded.

"What's wrong with letting her take it off?" my dad innocently inquired. "She's little; nothing is showing."

I remember standing among the beans and peas, straining my neck to keep my head up as I watched the ping-pong discussion of what was and was not okay and what I should and should not be allowed to do. I distinctly remember the sinking feeling of being the loser in this female-versus-male match. Mom won and my shirt stayed on. Only being about four years old, I was quick to surmise that my brother had a distinct advantage. It seemed boys and girls were different in some way, and things may not be equal. In that moment, I felt utter disappointment, and I resented my brother and my mom. It was an innocent moment, but my feelings around how I experienced it would turn into a strongly-held belief. That instance was the beginning of an internal struggle, slowly welling up, a belief of being the lesser gender. It was a deep groove in the vinyl record of my life of a memory that would play over and over again as I began to observe and question other instances of perceived injustice between boys and girls, men and women, males and females. My thoughts and feelings I associated with those instances turned into a deep-rooted, entrenched belief. Did this have something to do with not making vice president?

Jumping forward to 2018, my last year working for the utility where I had spent thirty-nine years, I had created a collage at the prompting of one of my mentees. I had done vision boards in the past, but did not keep them. The one I made at her urging still hangs on the wall in my art studio. It contains pictures and words from some of my favorite magazines of architecture, fashion, and travel. On it also hangs tapestry swatches and metal charms representing my overseas adventures. It also portrays some powerful words and phrases in bold such as, “In the Land of Men,” “Nevertheless She Persisted,” and “Don’t Tell Me I Can’t.” These words came to mind as I was writing. For most of my life I have been pushing against men and their corporate rules, believing I (a female) am the lesser gender. I have spent my lifetime needing to prove myself. I desperately wanted to prove men wrong about the beliefs I attributed to them, of my inferiority. This negative belief is a form of resistance that does not serve me. My deep-seated belief was that men had an advantage in corporate America, and I needed to struggle and claw my way to obtain similar accomplishments in their world. Seeing my collage one year later with those words and pictures, elicited a poignant reaction. There was definitely a theme to my thoughts, and it came from a place of limiting beliefs. This realization made me feel sheepish. Why did I believe, not just think, but truly believe, I was somehow less than others, especially men?

I believe it started in the garden. I believe I took my interpretation of that instance and subconsciously decided to look at the world through that lens, through the belief I created about it. From that moment in my adolescence, I started looking for things, behaviors, words and actions that reinforced that belief. Guess what? I found them, lots of them.

Looking for messages that matched my belief is similar to all of a sudden seeing advertisements for new washing machines, once my washing machine died. Because my antenna was up in terms of needing to find a replacement washer, it seemed that all the ads on television, in the newspaper and online shouted at me that my new washer was out there, in many styles, colors and loaded with features. Those same ads were there all along, but because I was not focused on that need, I did not see them.

This is the same with our thoughts. When coupled with strong feelings, thoughts can turn into beliefs. We think a thought over and over. Each time we think the thought, our feelings usually get stronger, and with enough focus, the thought becomes a belief.

CHAPTER 2

INNATE GIFTS

As a result, a life of proving myself equal started to grow. The feeling of that day in the garden came with me when I entered first grade at barely six years old. That first year away from home and the security of my mom and dad was peppered with the influence of those in power. Those who I perceived as wise and all-knowing.

My journey through grade school revealed a few natural gifts. Some of my early grade-school teachers quickly realized those gifts could help them teach more effectively and could possibly help my classmates at the same time. Making others feel valued and helping them discover their self-worth are gifts I continue to humbly share with everyone.

I remember Mom squatting down in front of me as she explained what my first day of first grade would be like. The top of my seemingly large desk was just below my chin. She spoke in a calm, reassuring tone that she would be back at the end of the day to pick me up. I was reminded to be polite, mind my teacher and say please and thank you, and then she left. Wait a minute! What? She was leaving me in this place? I instantly felt sick. Did I mention one of my family-designated nicknames was "worrywart?" That feeling of abandonment coupled with being terrified of my first-grade teacher resulted in my becoming suddenly ill several times throughout first grade. Mom could never figure out why I miraculously recovered once I got home. I finally confessed to her in fourth grade that I was deathly afraid of my first-grade teacher.

I was raised to respect my elders and especially those in a place of power (importance). I was not to question them; I was to obey. I think being raised as a staunch Catholic had something to do with that belief. It was easy to obey the nuns who taught us because they were formidable. They wore floor-length heavy, black, wool robes, belted at the waist by a rope-like rosary. To make them even more uncomfortable, they had to wear tight, forehead-creasing, jaw-binding black and white habits that wrapped tightly around their head and neck. The priests also dressed in black. No wonder they never seemed very happy.

I remember two instances in first grade where by just being myself, I used my unbeknownst talents. One of the boys in my class always seemed to be causing trouble. He could not seem to sit still and was routinely disrupting the teacher's lessons for the day. I remember Sister Mary Francis, the nun I was petrified of, talking with me one day saying she was going to move my desk next to his. She asked that I try to help him focus more and minimize his disruptions. I remember a little bit about how that worked out, and I did seem to help him somewhat. Sometimes he just wanted to talk and be noticed. Looking back, I think he needed to feel valued, paid attention to, and sometimes he also needed help with his school work. I also remember the teacher telling me to help other students with some of their work. I do not remember in what subjects I tried to help, but I do remember finding it easy, almost second-nature, as if I could sense what they needed. My words and actions seemed to flow out of me like a fluid waterfall, spilling into a quiet pond. I was raised with the words "We are all made in God's image and likeness." I assume it was my inner me, my God-image, speaking and acting through my physical me. I was not special, but I liked helping. I was just this little girl with wavy hair and slanted bangs. Good thing my mom-cut hair had nothing to do with the gifts and desires of my heart.

The other classmate I remember being moved next to was a petite girl with big brown eyes. She was this lovely, dark-haired, silent beauty. She spoke when spoken to, but rarely initiated conversation with others. Sister Mary Francis wanted to see if I could bring her out of her shell, so to speak. I remember her printing was so artistic. It was really calligraphy, and she was only a first-grader. I tried to copy it because it was so beautiful and unique. To me, her quietness was if she was much wiser than all of us and she had to sit out her time in this classroom with a bunch of talkative, energized six- and seven-year-olds. Thinking back, she seemed like an old soul in a young body. I came to adore her, her unique style, and her sweet shyness. Sometimes after school I would go home with her where she would show me all the art work and embroidery she was learning and the sewing her mom was teaching her. In my eyes, she was so talented and yet she had no idea she was. We were very close friends all through the eight years of grade school. I still have some of the things she made me—Raggedy Ann and Andy dolls and a cool '70s jeans purse made out of the back pockets. I guess I helped her some by making her laugh, by making light of myself, by trying to help her see how uniquely talented she was and also by being her friend. I appreciated her for exactly who she was. What I remember was sensing her unease and shyness and wanting her to know she was perfect, absolutely perfect, just the way she was. She also helped me by encouraging me to discover my own artistic style.

This desire of wanting everyone to feel valued remains strong in me today. Also, needing to feel valued would drive my efforts to rise up the corporate ladder. Not only did I want those who were in places of power to acknowledge my value, I wanted every employee to feel valued. I believed it was leadership's responsibility, as well as my own, to make people feel appreciated.

Other lessons from my adolescent journey were believing what my folks told me, especially my mom, respecting and almost being fearful of adults in power, like my teachers. Dad and Mom were opposites. Mom saw life through rose-colored glasses and Dad believed in the school of hard knocks. His childhood reflected the idea that the education life gives you comes from sacrifice and pain from mostly negative experiences. Mom, though, loved being with people, really could not cook and I do not think really liked any of the expected housewife (women's work) duties and responsibilities of the 1950s and 1960s. Dinner was expected to be on the table when the working husband arrived home. The house was to be neat and tidy, the children playing quietly, the clothes cleaned and put away and a general sense of tranquility when the bread-winner stepped through the door. Not! I do not fault Mom. She liked business and being out in the world of men, challenging her brain and interacting with lots of people. I grew up liking the same.

Mom used to tell me I could be anything I wanted. Dad would add, "As long as you don't step on anyone on your way up." With those words and much love, I grew up with some self-confidence in my future, tempered with humility and respect and never judging someone because I had not walked a mile in their moccasins. This was a Native American pearl of wisdom that was etched into a small piece of Ponderosa pine, with the bark carved out and a hook attached, that held Mom's wedding rings when she washed dishes. At times I was like my mom, positive and outgoing. At other times, I was like my dad, shy and reserved. I find it interesting how moments in my life, moments that only lasted minutes, influenced how I saw the world and my interpretation of my place in it. Those moments were thoughts in my head, with feelings I experienced at the time. The more I thought them and felt them, the more real they became, until they were beliefs. At the time, I did not understand that process. I did not realize I was choosing what to believe.

For some reason, and to this day I do not know why, I was self-confident in front of crowds. No matter how big or small, I loved being in front of them. This became obvious even in first grade. I always raised my hand, more like waved my hand, to speak in front of the class about what I had done over summer vacation. Public speaking was fun to me. You may be thinking, *what an odd little kid.* You might even think I was not normal, and my brother and sisters would probably agree with you! It was who I was, and who I am today. I am an odd combination of shyness and showmanship, especially demonstrated in my younger years. With someone older and in authority, I pretty much kept my mouth shut. Contrast that with an opportunity to perform in front of others, and I was the first one to volunteer.

Every year my grade school held a talent show where parents and grandparents could come see their sweet darlings perform. Picture it. I was barely six years old in first grade. I was dressed in my Catholic school uniform, a blue-gray plaid, wool bib-top jumper with matching skirt, a short-sleeved white Peter Pan collar cotton blouse, blue knee highs and my one pair of school shoes. Saddle shoes were the rage in those days. I loved the two-toned leather, low white oxford with the contrasting black overlapping piece for the laces. That black cutout resembled a horse saddle. The picture would not be complete without a description of my slanted bangs. Because money was tight, Mom regularly cut all of our hair. Mom would cut my hair when it was wet. She had a bad tendency of pulling down my bangs, pressing them tight to my forehead and proceeding to cut them straight across. As my wavy hair dried, so did the bangs, which ended up much shorter than I liked. That straight-across cut resulted in angled bangs that looked like an ocean wave engulfing the beach. Until getting a professional cut in eighth grade, my haircuts were traumatic for me. I ended up sobbing in my room, because I hated how home-cut my hair always looked.

For this first talent show, I decided to sing a song, a cappella! I had heard a song on the radio that summer before first grade. It was performed in French, "Freya Jacques." If you want a chuckle, check it out on your favorite internet search engine. I could only remember the chorus. Do you ever remember hearing a prayer, a saying or a song when you were little and repeating what you thought you heard, only to be surprised to learn later that what you heard and remembered were not the exact words? Well that was how I memorized the French words I thought I heard for the chorus of "Freya Jacques."

Dad was able to see me perform that afternoon. He must have been working in town then, because rarely could he attend any of our school or our few athletic events. Being a sheet-metal mechanic, he mostly worked on new construction. Spokane, my hometown, was not a fast-growing, bustling city at that time which meant he worked out of town most of the time. Dad was in the very back of the school auditorium; it was where he felt most comfortable. He did not like the limelight, nor did he enjoy visiting with folks. Not wanting to be noticed, Dad slipped into his seat in the back just before the show started.

As I walked out onto the stage, I remember the spotlights being so bright I could only make out silhouette shapes in front of me. My classmates were there, also some of their siblings, parents and grandparents. From my dim view, it looked like a packed house. I was hoping Dad was among them. Mom usually found a way to attend most of our school events. My memory is definitely clear about standing on that big stage alone but surprisingly, not afraid. I found the moment curious, though, as it was my first time on a stage, and the feeling of the bright lights and all eyes on me, gave me pause. Dad's recollection was much different. He told me later that he was nervous for me.

As I stood there, staring, and nothing coming out of my mouth, Dad said he anxiously mumbled to himself, "She's not gonna sing. She's not gonna sing." Then to his surprise and relief, I started to sing. I was singing a song, a cappella, in words that sounded French to me. It was definitely my rendition. Since I only knew the chorus, my debut was very short. I finished singing and walked off the stage as if walking out the door after another day at work. It was no big deal. I had done what I came to do, and that was that.

I do not remember winning anything, but I do remember the sense of accomplishment, hearing the applause as I left the stage. Reliving the thought of those people clapping and the feeling of success in that moment, turned into a desire and then a belief. I believed I had some kind of talent or something they liked, and I looked forward to competing every year through eighth grade. Sometimes I would perform with a group of girls. In sixth grade, three of my friends and I lip-synched to a popular '70s song with fake drums, a real electric keyboard (unplugged, of course), and a cardboard cutout electric guitar. In seventh grade the same four of us twirled our batons, performing an original routine set to "I Feel the Earth Move" by Carole King.

Mostly, I liked competing by myself, because I had no one to blame if I did not win. I tended to be a perfectionist in everything I did, so being the best was always the goal. Placing second or third felt like losing. In eighth grade I remember playing my six-string acoustic guitar and singing. I remember messing up during my performance. I forgot some of the words, but I did not let it trip me up; I just sang the chorus again like that was exactly how I planned it. Cool as a cucumber!

I remember competing for a spot on the cheerleading squad when I attended our local community college. I decided, somewhat last minute, to compete. I chose "Sir Duke" by Stevie Wonder, a fast-paced pop song. As tryout got closer, I was nervous because I kept messing up on correctly repeating all the moves for the chorus. Then I remembered, who will notice if I mess up? It is not like I have another person performing with me. So, I kind of winged it. The good news was, I made the cheerleading squad. The bad news was, each cheerleader was to teach the other members their tryout routine. I panicked, but my panic was short-lived. None of the other cheerleaders wanted to learn my routine, because there were so many moves in it and the music was so fast. Whew! I digress.

Jan, my sister, was the musical and thespian prodigy in our house, but we did not compete together in grade school. I was the little sister. For those of you who have younger siblings, there are times in childhood when hanging out with a little sister is not cool. She was three years older, and she and I were not interested in doing the same things, anyway. I always seemed to be working on creating something or finding ways to make money, and that is not what girls my age spent their time doing. I already knew I was different, by the way I looked and acted, and never fit with the in-crowd.

Even though I was self-confident performing on stage and having the ability to help people get out of their shell, I was very shy in other ways. Sometimes I was so shy I would not go up to the counter of the local hamburger joint to ask for extra ketchup packets. Dad would try to coax me, “Go up and ask nicely.” I was too afraid, too self-conscious, and so I would go without. I think it had to do with being taught to respect your elders—which I often translated into fearing them.

I have always been an average athlete. I loved the water and successfully competed in local swim meets at ages twelve and thirteen. My first water incident was when I was about two years old. I jumped off the edge of the public swimming pool near the deep end, unbeknownst to my mom who had turned her head for just a minute to watch one of my siblings. I popped up coughing and spitting but did not seem afraid, or so I have been told by the numerous stories belabored by Donna, Tommy, and Jannie about my behavior in the summer when Dad worked out of town in Pullman, Washington. Pullman is a college town, home to Washington State University. We rented a small place to be with Dad, instead of him having to drive the 180 miles roundtrip. I am surprised I survived those summer road trips, according to my sisters and brother. They complained about me crying all the way down and all the way back, in the heat of the summer in our early '60s green station wagon, with no air conditioning, four kids, two adults and Lucky, our black Labrador, panting and slobbering all over everything and everyone. I think I was crying because I sensed all three of them wanting to accidentally get rid of me at a bathroom stop! I do remember the playpen Mom caged me in during the day when my siblings were playing games or playing with their toys. I hated being trapped behind those bars. I remember my little fists, glued to the playpen rails, shaking them and wailing to get out. Once I was determined, look out.

I was reminded of the tall slide in the local park in Pullman. The summers were hot and the metal slide got sticky from the sweaty legs of all the kids going down it. Donna said they figured out that sitting on wax paper would help you zoom down the slide. I apparently was not thrilled to go down the slide with Donna, until she put wax paper under us. Donna said I became a holy terror after that first run, because I kept trying to climb the ladder to the top to go down again. Donna's fun was cut short, having to keep an eye on her baby sister.

There was one time during the 1962 World's Fair in Seattle, Washington, when Donna and I went on a ride called the Wild Mouse. It was a maze of tracks, similar to a roller coaster but shaped like a square pyramid with little cars you sat in that turned abruptly at each corner. As the tandem car edged its way to the top of the ride, there were no railings to help stop the car if it came off the tracks. I can remember thinking,

I'm done with this ride, unbuckling the thinly worn leather belt and starting to get out of the ride as it edged toward a sharp corner. I think the only reason Donna, sitting behind me, was screaming at me and trying to shove me back in my seat, as Mom and Dad watched in terror below, was that she was more afraid of Mom and Dad "killing" her if she did not come back with me in one piece! Fortunately for Donna, she got off the ride with me in tow and in one piece. Again once I made up my mind, determination got the best of me.

We all learned to snow ski at a young age. With money being so tight, we only went up to Mt. Spokane, the local ski resort, a few times each year. Dad would save his silver dollars in an empty coffee tin. When I asked if we had enough to go, he would get the tin down from the top of his and mom's closet and pry open the plastic lid. If he could shake it and there was still lots of room for more silver coins, he would say, "Not quite enough!" We could not afford ski lessons, so our lessons entailed Dad clamping on our skis and giving us a shove down the hill. I came up with the wild belief that good skiers did not need to use their poles. One day on the bunny hill at Mt. Spokane, there were a bunch of skiers lined up across the path down to the rope tow, taking a group ski lesson. Since I did not have my poles and really did not know how to ski very well, turn appropriately or stop quickly, I came barreling down the hill towards the long line of skiers. I remember seeing the terror on a few faces as I rapidly approached them, not slowing down. I would have plowed into at least a couple of them head-on had they not parted like the Red Sea in the Bible. They fell over like dominos. Being so small, I easily slipped between the space left from them falling on top of one another. The instructor was yelling profanities and Dad was appalled as he watched from the top of the hill, with everyone wondering whose little terror I was. Needless to say, I had to use my poles from then on.

To some degree, even at a young age, I must have naturally believed we all had some control over our thoughts, feelings and beliefs. A couple of instances are still with me. The first has to do with a little girl about my age who lived down the block. One day she made me really mad. I remember storming into our house, plopping myself down on a chair and whining to Mom about her making me mad. My wise mom asked just one question, "So she made you mad?

I adamantly replied, "Yes!" what a lame question. Had I not just said that?

Then she calmly said, "If she truly made you mad, then she is in control of your emotions. Is she in control?" What? No! What did this have to do with her making me mad? Why wasn't Mom taking my side and backing me up? Her point, as she went on to explain, was we choose how we act and react. If we let others influence these seemingly little things about our emotions or our beliefs, what about the big things, the more important things in our life? Did I want others to be in control of my fate? Heck no! I sort of understood what she was saying. Looking back on my life's journey, I should have put that into practice more instead of letting others upset me or feeling bad about something they said or did.

There was a similar instance when the power of my beliefs would be tested. I think I was maybe in sixth or seventh grade. There was a sleep-over at a classmate's house to celebrate a birthday. I was not fond of sleep-overs because I tended to always start feeling sick and then went home early. I think I feared being away from the security of how my mom made me feel when Dad was working out of town. I am assuming that if I thought about it long enough, I would find something that happened earlier in my life that influenced that need for security.

Sometimes I was able to talk myself out of throwing up. One time one of my other classmates was having similar symptoms. I sat with her and had her think of things that made her feel better. My goal was to get her focus off her thoughts that she was going to vomit. I do not remember all the things she and I talked about, but she started to feel better. Talking more positively with her made me feel better, too. However, I was being picked up soon by my mom, and my classmate did not want me to leave. I reassured her that she needed to keep thinking positive thoughts that made her feel good and to breathe and relax and she would be fine. She was fine until shortly after I left, then threw up. Why? I believe her thoughts and strong emotions took over. Before we started talking, she adamantly stated she was going to throw up. She believed it, so naturally what she focused on got bigger. Too bad I did not heed my own advice.

Though it seemed natural to be outgoing and help others, my shyness, and maybe insecurities, showed up in different ways. I have a strong memory of when I had to have my first cavity in a tooth filled. After my brother and sisters got a tooth or two filled, I remember walking down the sidewalk outside the dentist's office, holding Mom's hand. I wanted to know when I got to have one of those shiny things in my mouth! I still like shiny things, even if they have no monetary value.

When I had that first tooth filled, the syringe that was supposed to be filled with a numbing agent was filled with water. As the grinding began, an awful smell of a hot filling being drilled into my tooth ensued; I was squirming in the chair. The dentist kept telling me to try to relax and quit gripping the arm of the chair so tight. Even though I wanted to blurt out in pain, I thought this was the price you had to pay for getting one of those shiny things. The dentist was the expert; he was in the place of authority and power. When he was done, the dental hygienist was cleaning up the instruments and looked at the syringe in shock. She looked at me and asked if my mouth was numb. With tears in my eyes, I mumbled, "No."

"Why didn't you say something?" she demanded. "I used the wrong syringe; it only had water in it!" That is just one example of how shy I could be with adults who I believed were in control. I continued to be this blend of shyness and self-confidence, respecting (fearing) those in power and also helping those who needed a kind word or assistance to see their value in the hope it would help them believe in their self-worth.

As I continued through grade school, I observed my differences compared to my classmates. My beliefs about my body and how it should look were negative, and I am still a work in progress in that area.

I had naturally wavy, dishwater blonde hair with ash-blonde streaks. All the cool girls had long, straight hair. The really cool girls were petite and their hair was golden blonde. It did not help that I was also perceived as a goody two-shoes both at school and at home.

Tommy reminisced about me being a tattletale. Our basement was unfinished. We loved using it as our roller-skating rink, because you could skate all the way around the full basement. We used the open-framed walls as leverage for pulling ourselves from space to space. The floor was concrete and there were a couple of bedrooms that were partitioned off with cardboard between the wall studs. I liked riding my tricycle down there because the floor was smooth and did not contain any cracks or gravel, like the sidewalk outside. By the way, I had Dad spray-paint my red and white trike silver. Jannie used to stand on the back of my trike and would push with one foot to keep me moving fast because she added weight to my pedaling. Tommy and our cousin, Gary, who was the same age as Tommy, were shooting arrows with their bows at one of the cardboard walls and barely missing Jannie and me as we flew by. The arrow tips were really dull and barely stuck in the cardboard walls. One time as Jannie and I zipped around, Tommy accidentally hit Jannie in the back. I remember the gifted actor grabbing the arrow that stuck out of her shirt and wailing like she was dying. As Tommy recalled it, I scrambled off the trike and ran up the stairs. As he tried to catch me before I made my way to the top to tell on him to Mom, he said it was like trying to catch a greased pig! I was yelling at the top of my lungs, "Mom, Mom, Tommy hit Janet with an arrow!" Jan was fine, and her acting ability was confirmed. Tommy was pretty annoyed with me being a tattletale.

Being taller, more broad-shouldered and curvier than the other girls my age reinforced my feeling of being different from the norm. I remember being the first one in my class to get a bra in fourth or fifth grade. I was mortified. I remember Mom telling me I needed one because my body was changing. I could tell these kinds of conversations made Mom uncomfortable. It seemed her beliefs about her own body and the facts of life were either negative or uncomfortable to discuss. I quickly perceived that and thus believed the same.

I remember her taking me to a local department store located in the basement of a variety store in the outdoor neighborhood shopping center. Initially, she had a clerk help us. Mom was in the dressing room with me. I was embarrassed; I did not want a bra. It was another thing that marked me as different.

Mom was trying to make sure it fit me properly. Once I got it on, I could not figure out how to reach around to my back and hook it. Mom showed me a secret of doing that before you got it all the way on. Mom's brassieres were long-lined, with stays and underwire. She had become proficient in hooking hers from the back. Mom was endowed with plenty, as was Grandma Nicol, her mom. I was destined to be "blessed" in the same way, which I loathed.

Anyway, I remember we bought two bras, both white. One had a tiny pink bow on it and the other had a blue bow on it. When I got home and it was time for dinner, I remember being extremely self-conscious. Naturally, it was the talk at dinner, which embarrassed me even more.

I have the best brother in the whole world, and I have told this same story over and over again. Remember, he is seven years older and was in high school at the time. I usually wore his hand-me-down clothes, because

I was larger than my two older sisters. His outgrown clothes fit me the best. I liked his clothes anyway, because I was somewhat of a tomboy.

I distinctly remember that discussion at dinner. I was wearing his maroon hand-me-down shirt. I did not want to talk about the new bra. He tried to make me feel better, as he always did and still does. He said the other girls in my class would be jealous. I innocently asked why. He said I would understand as I got older, but this was a thing all girls wanted. Oh, so this was not the worst thing that had happened to me at this point in my life? Feeling a little more at ease, I lifted my shirt and said, "See the pretty bow on it!"

Mom instantly scolded, "Patty, pull your shirt down this instant!" We all had a laugh, but I will always remember how he made me feel so much better and less embarrassed. He continues to be that same lovable, caring big brother. As a side note, that night I walked into the shower with my bra still on, not yet used to this added undergarment.

As I went through the first eight grades of my academic life, I remember believing I could accomplish any goal and all my dreams. Conversely, I also had a strong opposing belief of needing to prove myself as a female, directly because of the inferior feeling I got during the garden incident. Without realizing it, I chose to continue this inner struggle until that day at fifty-nine years of age when Michele posed that life-changing question, "What if your belief the VP was holding you back was the reason you did not reach your goal?" I never questioned the belief that I was good at performing in front of a crowd, nor did I question or realize my career success was also based on my beliefs.

It is so interesting to look back on my life as if it is a movie playing out on a screen. When I wanted to learn to play a six-string guitar, I had no doubt I could do it and in a short amount of time. One Monday while in seventh grade, our teacher asked for a show of hands of those who wanted to play guitar for church service that coming Sunday. Though I had never played the guitar, my hand immediately shot up. *How hard could it be,* I briefly thought. There were only a handful of songs I needed to learn, and I had the perfect person to teach me in six days, my musically gifted sister, Jan. She learned to play so many instruments. She played guitar, cello, flute, trumpet, bass guitar—and the list goes on. She was and still is so talented. She even played the big pipe organ in church one Sunday, and she was only in first grade! She was too short to reach the pedals, which add depth to the music, so one of the nuns sat next to her and took care of them. The great part about learning to play guitar was that the guitar group stood in front of the congregation, and I was part of that group on Sunday.

CHAPTER 3

VALUES AND HIGH STANDARDS

My strong desire to make others feel valued played out many times in grade school. In instances where I thought those with legitimate power violated the responsibility that comes with that power and used it coercively, I did not shy away from standing up and speaking out. It seemed to come naturally.

My eighth-grade teacher was a nun. I perceived her as cranky with an exaggerated sense of self-worth. Earlier I would have attributed some of her negativity to how strict and uncomfortable nuns' religious habits (headgear) were. However, their wardrobe began to change by 1973. They were now wearing knee-length black dresses and light-weight veils which barely hung down to the top of their shoulders. Some of the more progressive nuns did not wear a veil at all. This relaxed wardrobe change did not seem to improve this nun's demeanor, however.

Sister Margaret did not garner our respect but rather demanded it, which rubbed me the wrong way. Even though she bragged of her various academic degrees, she did not know how to manage twelve- to thirteen-year-old teenagers. One day, in a tirade, she boldly proclaimed there would be no one who would teach us, because we were so unruly. Having already found my voice, especially with her, I instantly raised my hand and piped up that my mom would be delighted to come teach us. Sister Margaret was infuriated with that comment. She immediately dispatched me to the principal's office. "Go ahead, call your mom!" she said in disgust.

Mom had previously substituted as a teacher at our grade school. She had also been a typing and shorthand instructor at Spokane's Kinman Business University. Before that, she taught at the Spokane Technical and Vocation School (later to be named Spokane Community College) where she met my dad when he returned to school after World War II.

Anyway, Mom agreed and came to school the next morning. For the most part, my classmates respected Mom. She was strict and always fair. The old saying,

"She has eyes in the back of her head," definitely described Mom. One day while Mom was substitute teaching, one of my classmates threw a pencil eraser across the room at someone while Mom had her back to us, writing on the chalkboard. Without missing a beat and not even turning around, Mom said, "Go pick it up, Tony." We all gasped in delight!

There was one of my eighth-grade classmates who always seemed to get into trouble. Once, Sister Margaret accused him of doing something I knew he had not done. She was going to expel him from school. I annoyed her, once again, by defending him. I remember the issue going in front of the school principal and our parish priest. Because I was known as a goody two-shoes and never lied, my classmate was found innocent. This made Sister Margaret look a bit foolish, and she was visibly angry she could not expel him. My belief of doing the right thing by standing up, speaking out and telling the truth no matter the consequences, was deeply ingrained.

This dichotomy of self-confidence and shyness continued to reveal itself. In one moment, I was Joan of Arc riding her steed swinging her sword in the name of truth and justice. In the next moment I was a shy little girl, almost afraid of her shadow. My desire to be the voice of value for those who could not voice their own value grew stronger.

I want to make a point here that even when I dislike what others do, it does not mean I will disrespect them. I was reminded by one of my classmates that I stood up one day in class and told the group not to be so mean to Sister Margaret. I do not remember saying that, but it does sound like something I would say, even though Sister Margaret regularly annoyed me by misusing her authority and power.

I used my voice for proving others worthy, including myself. I continued needing to prove I was equal to the boys. One way to strengthen this equality belief was to rise above whenever I could. Getting straight A's in grade school was one of those ways. I stood out and rose above my male classmates and almost all of my female classmates. This belief went from a goal to an obsession. Straight A's turned into a lifelong struggle with perfectionism. Needing to feel valued and equal drove everything I did. Even though none of us will ever be perfect, to me, falling short of it seemed like a failure.

My mom and dad had some dichotomous beliefs. Mom believed in the ideal; we kids should uphold the family name, behave, mind our manners and our elders.

She was always pushing us to be our best. Dad believed he was flawed, so he wanted us to play more and have fun while we were children. He did not put emphasis on getting it right every time or trying to be perfect. Dad told us stories of how he had been ridiculed and bullied (my interpretation) by his first-grade teacher. He had dyslexia, a learning disorder that causes letters and numbers to get transposed. This makes it hard to recognize short, familiar words or to sound out longer words. He would often transpose telephone numbers or rearrange letters in someone's name. In the 1920s and '30s, people with dyslexia were viewed as stupid or lazy because it was not understood by most. In those days math and English were stressed and that meant numbers and letters, which Dad could not always read or write in the correct order. Consequently, and very unfortunately, Dad felt and believed he was stupid. He believed he was not worthy of anything or equal to anyone. I can see how he believed this, because that one teacher reinforced it by forcing Dad to sit on a tall stool in the front of the room with a dunce cap on. This was a form of humiliating punishment for both misbehaving and for failing to demonstrate proficiency in school work. This unkind act reinforced Dad's belief of his unworthiness, and it affected his entire life. He held this belief so strongly that up to his dying day at almost ninety-two years old, he still spoke of his unworthiness because he was not smart like everyone else. It hurt me to hear my dad restate that belief over and over again throughout his life, because it was not true. In his sheet-metal profession, Dad was always chosen for the complex jobs that required precision and artistic ability. We could never convince Dad of his intelligence and worth. From one of my overseas adventures, I had bought a painting that I wanted hung on my bedroom wall above the headboard of my bed. Some things, like hanging a picture, I do not take the time nor want to be patient enough to get it perfect. I would eyeball it and pound in the nail. Dad on the other hand, started asking me all kinds of precision-measurement questions. Did I want it centered from wall to wall, window to window or centered above the headboard? He used a measuring tape but then proceeded to do the complex fractions in his head. I was lost in the first fraction subtraction! I pointed this out, but his belief was so ingrained that he shrugged off my comment of his impressive mathematical skills. Our beliefs are the reasons why our life is playing out as it is. Our beliefs affect every aspect of our life. What thoughts and beliefs do you hold as true that may be nothing more than a thought you thought about and thought about, until it became a belief?

My adolescent journey was shaped by my thoughts, feelings and beliefs. As I progressed from a Catholic grade school (first to eighth grade) to a Catholic high school (ninth to twelfth grade), I brought all of my self-made beliefs with me. I brought my self-confidence in performing, my goal of perfectionism and my belief of needing to prove myself equal to men.

The all-girls private Catholic high school I attended was one of two small schools for girls in Spokane. I continued to work hard and had perfect attendance, from second grade to the beginning of my sophomore year. Remember, I was deathly afraid of my first-grade teacher, and that fear was the reason I missed school that year. I did not mention that she used to threaten to lock us up if we misbehaved. The jail cell was a wooden storage cage attached to the bottom of the fire escape. I was so afraid of her and her authority that one day, I even confessed to throwing away half of a sandwich at lunch just because she scared me into it! I had not thrown away any food. Her threatening to lock us up was enough to scare this little six-year-old into subservience. I had not found my voice in that first year in school, but standing up and speaking out would develop over time.

In the early part of my sophomore year, I developed a fever of 102 degrees and went to school anyway. I desperately wanted to have perfect attendance in high school. My teacher, concerned I could infect others, did not care about my perfect attendance goal and sent me home. I thought, felt and believed I had failed by not attaining that goal. Perfectionism continued to influence everything in my life, both professionally and personally.

Though I could never be perfect, I would excel in many areas in high school. While at the all-girls school, I remember staying up extremely late many nights in order to keep studying, keep reaching for straight A's and top scores. It was my mom's nightly routine to come into my room after I had gone to bed, to say good night and tuck me in. What she did not know was that I routinely hid school books under my blankets. When she left after saying good night, I would turn on a flashlight and return to studying. One particular night she sat on the edge of my bed when tucking me in, and my Spanish book slid out from under the covers.

At the time, Mom was the bookkeeper for the school. She knew and had access to all of my teachers, both the nuns and the few Catholic laity faculty, as nuns referred to them. Though the term means ordinary members of the Catholic Church who are not a nun nor a priest, apparently the nuns questioned the expertise of these non-clergy instructors. I treated the lay faculty with the same level of respect I gave to the nuns and priests. My dad used to caution me about feeling superior just because of possessing post-secondary education degrees. Dad said a college degree is just another tool in your life tool box, like experience. All life tools carry equal weight. When the books slid onto the floor, Mom immediately went to our rotary-dial phone and called my Spanish teacher, informing her I was staying up too late studying and worrying. She then handed the phone to me. My Spanish teacher told me to quit studying. She reassured me that I knew the material, and that I would do well on the exam the next day. This made me feel a little better and provided me a reason to quit studying and to go to sleep. Looking back, sleep was probably what I needed most, in order to get an A. I held myself to high standards in all things. I have always been hard on myself to be the best. The accolades I received for a 4.0 grade reinforced my self-worth.

Reflecting on those early years and my life today, I feel fortunate for the positive influencers in my life. My parents, grandparents, siblings and my few close friends. Throughout my life I have never had more than a couple of close female friends. My life events did not dovetail with the life events of most women my age. I have always been very focused on my goals of succeeding and being productive.

As a youngster, I remember Mom and Dad forcing me to go outside to play in the summer afternoons. Mornings were reserved for chores, both inside and out. I viewed playing mostly as a waste of time, as it accomplished nothing of value. Working with ceramics, creating jewelry and experimenting with other crafts have always interested me. I viewed these as productive, because I had something to show for the time spent. As my life experience continues, I am focusing more on the journey and not so much on the destination. I find something new to be grateful for every day. As I live through life's transitions and especially experiencing the passing of loved ones, cherishing today, this moment, becomes more important. As I sometimes remind myself, this exact moment is only and always now.

There was also an all-boys Catholic high school. As you can imagine, the girls, me included, wanted any excuse to be involved with the boys. Well, the school just happened to have a marching band for which the girls could audition. This was a legitimate way to go over to the boys' school during school hours. Jan already played trumpet, so I needed to pick a different instrument to learn to play so I could audition. Being true to my odd-man out, unconventional self, I chose the trombone. Why? I had rarely seen girls playing that instrument. I had to quickly take a few lessons the month before school started in order to audition. I could only take four lessons, but that did not stop me from believing I would get accepted. After my audition, I was informed I made second chair. First chair is the best player of the section and is also the leader of the section. Surprisingly, I was satisfied with being second chair. The pressure of being first chair did not interest me, because I did not want to make time to take more lessons.

I am not sure what continues to come over me to have such confidence in my ability to quickly learn something new and not be afraid to perform in front of others. Thinking about it now, I think I was focused on what I wanted, the goal. I wanted to be in the band with the boys, and I needed to play an instrument. I was not worried, nor gave much thought to this type of unknown. I had my eyes on the end game, performing in front of large audiences sounded exciting, and I was determined to get into the marching band no matter what.

CHAPTER 4
FOLLOWING IN THEIR FOOTSTEPS

In the middle of my sophomore year, I switched from the all-girls Catholic high school to a public school to broaden my course choices. The public school was located in a poorer suburb of Spokane. I remember that very first day at my new school. Mom came into the school office with me to make sure all my classes were lined up for the rest of the school year, since it was mid-year.

The first class of each day was homeroom. This was a class in which students assembled with their homeroom teacher before dispersing to other classes. School announcements were made, notices to students were delivered, etc. My homeroom was on the top floor of the 1932 brick building about a quarter of the way down the hall. Homeroom had already started, so there were no students in the hall, just me. Mom accompanied me to the third floor but stayed back, standing on the top of the staircase, as I timidly proceeded down the hall. When I reached the door of my homeroom, I looked back at her, seemingly petrified to open that door into this new world of learning and new friends.

I remember nervously holding the big round brass door handle in my sweaty hand. I was so focused on the knob; it was all I could see. I remember hearing nothing, but the pounding of my heart. I remember saying to myself, "Just open the door. Just open the door." I looked back at Mom, who was smiling assuredly, and I opened the door. This was the beginning of many happy memories, new opportunities and my first boyfriend, the drum major of the marching band.

Public high school is where I blossomed in terms of music. At home, Mom would find ways to reinforce skills that benefited more than one thing. Being that she was a typing and shorthand teacher, she felt we needed to learn to type. When Mom decided I should take piano lessons while still in grade school, typing became a way to strengthen my fingers, especially my little fingers. Manual typewriter keys definitely took finger strength. Mom said typing would make me a better pianist. This was the same routine for all four of us kids. I also think she wanted us to have plenty to keep us busy, especially during the summer, so we would stay out of her hair. I was very interested in learning shorthand, so she taught me that, too. I knew how to type and take some shorthand before I entered public high school. I continue to be an overachiever.

I enjoyed all the music offerings at my new school. There was an elite jazz singing group whose members were selected through an audition. The selections were based on singing ability and on personal character. I believe I was chosen more based on the latter. It was a big deal or rather it was made to feel like a big deal to be selected. The way you found out if you made it after your audition, was a few of the seniors in the group would come to your house and wake you up really early in the morning by singing. You had to stay in your pajamas as they kidnapped you to a local restaurant for breakfast. Of course, parents knew what was happening. I was so excited, because I was a junior then and was still relatively unknown to everyone. Most of my classmates had attended elementary school and junior-high school together. So, off to the restaurant and still in our pajamas, to find out who else made it in the group. I had so much fun learning jazz and harmonizing, making new friends and competing in jazz festivals in Washington and Oregon. I loved the pre-stage jitters and performing in front of large audiences. What fond memories.

One of the main reasons I switched high schools was the lack of business courses offered at the all-girls school. I was not interested in the humanities, which was the focus of the Catholic school. I was curious about business. Both of my older sisters had also transferred to the same public high school; Donna at the beginning of her senior year, and Jannie at the middle of her junior year. I followed in the middle of my sophomore year. It was the best decision I made at that point in my life. Mom and Dad were very supportive even though the other Catholics in our parish and at the all-girls school thought what we were doing was a sin. They believed we were all going to hell. I admired how Mom and Dad handled the judging glances in church and the condescending comments. Both of my parents were strong individuals with a good sense of right and wrong. They were not concerned about us going to hell; thank goodness. Transferring to a public high school positively affected the trajectory of my life.

Having both of my sisters change high schools influenced my decision to follow in their footsteps. I have always idolized my oldest sister, Donna, who is nine years older than me. After high school, she went to Kinman Business University (KBU) in Spokane for some typing and secretarial classes, earning her a certificate in about ten months. She and another classmate were offered a job interview with an accounting firm while they were finishing up at KBU. She remembered telling the owner if he did not hire her, he would regret not having her on his team. Maybe I got some of my boldness from watching her. She dressed so stylishly when she went to work including occasionally wearing short wigs over her very long, dark brown hair. I wanted to be just like her in every way.

She was the reason I knew early on what I wanted to be when I grew up. I had made up my mind in grade school that I would pursue one of two professions: a nun or a secretary, like Donna. I liked the structure of what I thought a nun was and did. I was not thrilled that they were not allowed to dress up and could not voice their opinions. During the 1960s and early '70s, females were steered in the direction of only a handful of professions: homemaker, teacher, receptionist, secretary, nurse or librarian. At the time, these were the noble female professions that were deemed suitable.

When I started junior college in the fall of 1977, which was a two-year educational institution, girls did not have many nontraditional role models. There was no internet, just newspapers, television that only had four channels including the public broadcasting station and a handful of radio stations. The husband was the breadwinner, and the woman had the supporting roles of wife and/or raising the children. I loathed these stereotypes. It reminded me of the garden incident. I definitely was not interested in being stuck at home, raising kids, and had no desire of taking someone else's last name, if I ever got married.

I remember discussing what I wanted to be with my dad. Knowing I had narrowed it down to a nun and a secretary, he knowingly advised me, "I don't think you should become a nun. I think you oughta do you to the business world. They can probably handle you." We both laughed, knowing I was pretty comfortable being me.

Adults, especially people in authority, continue to hold a place of esteem and respect in my view. I unthinkingly default to them being all-knowing. They are older and should be wiser because of what they have learned and experienced both personally and professionally. I deeply believe there is no end to what can be learned and strive every day to be the best me.

My mom's mom was a profound role model for me and someone I viewed as experienced and hard working.

If you can imagine, she went through a divorce and remarried in the late 1940s, which was not the norm for women in her day. I am sure she was looked upon in disgust and as a failure, because she could not figure out how to be a good wife. She had also dropped out of school at the end of eighth grade, which was somewhat common in her time. Children needed to help their folks by either working around the home or getting a job. At age sixty, the same age I am today writing this book, she decided to go back to school to get her high-school diploma. She had to physically attend a continuation high school with mostly young adults. This school was primarily designed for girls who had gotten pregnant during their high school years and were kicked out of their regular high school. It was also for boys who were disinterested in their regular high-school classes and had dropped out or got kicked out. Grandma was the oldest student they ever had at the time. We still have her high-school graduation photograph; a black-and-white photo of her proudly smiling, holding her diploma. What a strong example of never give up and don't let anyone put you down.

As I considered my choices for a secretarial education, I wanted one where I got what I needed in the quickest time possible. I was anxious to get a good-paying job and join the ranks of the employed. Therefore, I planned on going to KBU just like my idol, Donna. I never gave any thought to attending a four-year institution. None of my family members graduated from a four-year college, so it never crossed my mind.

CHAPTER 5

HE CHANGED MY LIFE

I was all set and had paid my $100 registration fee to go to KBU. I had attended one typing class with Donna when she was going to school there, and I was still in grade school. I got to type on a typewriter in the back of the room. The teacher saw me erasing over the levers of the keys. This was a no-no because the eraser crumbs gummed up the levers and then the keys would stick while striking them with your fingers. The instructor was patient and kind when showing me how to erase correctly. It was such fun being with Donna. It was the feeling of being a secretarial student. I carried my small notebook as if I were carrying several textbooks. I literally followed in her footsteps, somewhat scared of all the adults, but proud to be her little sister. I remember being impressed with their modern vending machines that held miniature cans of soup, served piping hot. *How ingenious,* I thought!

Also, I got to spend part of a day with Donna at the job she was awarded over her classmate when she was finishing KBU. Her secretarial job seemed to be the linchpin of the organization, and Donna made it seem glamorous.

The summer immediately following my high-school graduation and before starting KBU, Mom needed to take her personal typewriter in for repairs. I decided to go with her. At Spokane Community College (SCC) they had a business-machines repair class taught by a dedicated instructor. I will never forget him, as his caring actions changed my life.

As he was looking over the typewriter, he inquired about my age and my school plans. When he found out I was planning to attend KBU, he said I needed to give SCC a chance. Graciously, Mom agreed to take the time for him to introduce me to some of the faculty. Since it was summer, there were not a lot of them around. He eagerly proceeded to drag me from classroom to classroom, finding instructors who were available to talk with me and tell me the myriad of reasons why I should attend SCC and not KBU.

In less than one hour, this quaint older gentleman changed my mind. The main reason he did was because he cared enough about one person, me. He wanted to show me what I would be missing by attending KBU. I felt valued as an individual and did not feel like a number, which was how I thought higher-education institutions viewed students. The next two years at SCC were just like what I experienced on that summer day with him. I had wonderful teachers who had real-world experience; they knew the latest skills and took care of the individual. I was not a social security number, I was Patty. I loved going to SCC, and I learned a great deal.

I had originally planned on only attending for one year and getting an executive secretarial certificate. Again, I was anxious to get out into the business world. I was more than ready to take on the world, but was the business world ready for me?

While attending that first year, I found out that if I stayed an additional year and took a few more classes, I could obtain an Associate of Applied Science (AAS) Executive Secretarial degree and an AAS Mid-Management degree. That seemed prudent. So instead of staying for twelve months, I stayed two years. During that time, I garnered a work-study position in the president's office in the afternoons after attending my classes. The woman I worked for became a very special friend. We remained good friends right up to her passing in 2019; she was eighty years young.

I idolized her just like I idolized Donna. She was the executive secretary to the president of the college. This was the highest position for a secretary there. She dressed to the nines and was professional along with being simply beautiful. I adored Sharran and was grateful for the positive impact she made on my life.

Working in the president's office, I would collect the mail from our mail room. Little did I know, but I would meet a young man who would become my best friend, confidant and what I could not recognize then, but do now, my soulmate. He also had a work-study job delivering the mail. I remember he was shy, but friendly. He, too, would join the electric and natural gas utility, and we would work side-by-side in the engineering department a few short years later. Nothing is a coincidence.

One of the extra-curricular clubs I joined in my second year was Delta Epsilon Chi (DEC) Honor Society. Distributive Education Club of America, DECA, as it is often referred to, is a career-technical student organization that prepares emerging leaders and entrepreneurs for careers in marketing, finance, hospitality and management in high schools and colleges around the globe. It is designed to combine work experience with classroom experiences. DEC stressed leadership and professionalism. DEC students got opportunities to lead, delegate, share, dream and succeed. Competition allowed club members to compete with students from other DEC chapters in the individual states in such areas as hotel/restaurant, tourism, human relations decision making and entrepreneurship. I joined my second (last) year at SCC. Competitions are held at the state level and then winners in each category compete at the national level. Because I was an industrious college student, always taking between 20-26 credits per quarter, I needed to compete in an area that did not require a great deal of prepared materials. I chose Human Relations (HR) Decision Making because the participant would be given an HR problem to solve in fifteen minutes and then orally present recommendations. Preparation to compete involved reading case studies and solving HR issues. I took first place in the state of Washington in that event, which qualified me for nationals in Houston, Texas.

There was an interesting philosophy my DEC advisor used on me the night before the national competition. He knew how nervous I was getting, and he surmised I would let that get in the way of demonstrating my best self. So, he talked with me about the next morning competition and basically said, "You are younger than most of the other competitors who have worked in the business world and have come back to school to obtain additional knowledge. You are not capable of beating them, so just go out there and have fun." BS! I got my hackles up and was determined to prove him wrong. How could he give me such a deflated speech? Why wasn't he pumping me up? To my surprise, he knew me very well. Had he praised me and my abilities, he knew I would shrug it off and not believe him. He knew if he challenged me, I would forget about being scared and would focus on proving him wrong; he was spot-on. My only focus was showing him I did know something and was equal to any of the other older and possibly wiser competitors. Fear subsided and the self-confidence of wanting to win took over. I took third place in the national competition. The awards ceremony reminded me of the Olympics, when the first-, second- and third-place finishers get up on podiums, a medal is hung around your neck and you are also given a trophy … a big trophy. When I came off the stage and back to the table we were all at, I all but shoved the trophy in his face. In disgust I uttered, "See, you didn't think I could do it!"

He chuckled a chuckle I had heard many times before. It was as if he knew something I did not. He smiled his Cheshire-cat grin and said, "I knew you could do it! I also knew you had to quit being fearful in order to be your best. I told you what you needed to hear." Proving myself equal and worthy had reared its head once again.

While continuing to take classes at SCC, I applied for a scholarship through the secretarial program. Part of the scholarship process involved each applicant competing in a mock interview conducted by various local employers. I was interviewed by a woman from the private, investor-owned, local electric and natural gas utility. She worked in a department involved with the natural gas side of the business.

While working one afternoon in the president's office at my work-study job, the head of employment for the utility contacted me asking if I would consider becoming an employee, specifically an executive secretary for one of their vice presidents. I was shocked and excited. I had planned on submitting my job application to the utility or to IBM, which my brother-in-law, Wayne, worked for at the time. Wayne worked for IBM for more than forty-five years, and I always admired his knowledge and problem-solving ability while in the middle of a crisis. He repaired a myriad of electronic business machines that had failed during a critical business need, like not being able to ring up sales during the Christmas rush, for example.

I responded, "Where did you get my name? How do you know who I am?" She informed me that the female employee who had participated in the mock interview was impressed with my skills and my interview. Little did I know, but that mock interview was the interview that would land me my first business position. My working relationship with the utility would last for more than thirty-nine years.

I finished the last of my classes, graduated summa cum laude that June, and went to work for the utility in August of 1979. I became what I had planned on becoming since I was very young, a secretary. This position was second only to the top secretarial position at the company, which was the executive secretary to the president/chief executive officer.

Utilities were very stable, which matched one of the values Dad had instilled in me when looking for a career. He and Mom had gone through the Great Depression, so they knew what it meant to have almost nothing and to constantly worry about their finances. They also saw many people lose their jobs and their homes. There was much suffering during those years, and Dad wanted more for us kids. An electric and natural gas utility was a stable place to work, and IBM was a prodigious corporation that had been in business a very long time. Either seemed like a good choice.

Accepting that executive secretarial position required I conform to a very conservative, gender-specific dress code. In 1979 those in positions of authority set the rules. Employees who decided to dress fashionably were frowned upon. Females were expected to wear a dress or a knee-length skirt and a blouse but nothing too flashy. I had bought one professional navy-blue two-piece business suit for the DEC competition, so at least I had that. Then I bought some very conservative, womanly dresses. I felt like I took my exuberant personality, dressed it in plain clothes and stuffed it in a brown paper bag. My bubbly personality was always fighting to get out!

CHAPTER 6

DREAM JOB?

I quickly realized why out of all the qualified secretaries at the company at the time, not one of them wanted this job. My nineteen-year-old self would describe my boss as creepy. I felt uncomfortable being around him. He drank regularly after hours and developed the habit of calling two of us younger subordinates at home. He never got too inappropriate, but he sounded like he had had plenty. There were only three of us, all female, who worked for him. He would call me and my coworker, who was just a couple of years older than me. I do not know if he ever called the eldest of us three in that stupor. She had been working for him for many years.

My coworker received so much harassment from him that she experienced anxiety. For me, I remember crying one Sunday night, hating the thought of having to go back to work for him the next day. After one of his evening weekend calls, my dad said, "Enough!" I was nineteen and still living with my parents.

I was already at work that next morning when he arrived. He called me into his office and sheepishly inquired, "So, I guess I called you last night?"

I promptly replied, "Yes."

He continued, "So I'm guessing I was inappropriate?"

Again, I said, "Yes" and followed it up with a warning that it should never happen again. He looked humiliated and embarrassed and a little worried and vowed it would not. I remember feeling extremely nervous, but I knew I had to speak up and express my disgust with his inappropriate words and actions. I wanted him to fear I would take action if he ever pulled something like that again.

Needless to say, my first professional working relationship with this boss was tumultuous. I hated every minute I was there and wanted to quit. He reinforced my deep-rooted belief that men thought they were superior to women and there was not much we, as females in their workplace, could do about it. He had me do nonwork-related errands like purchasing a gift for his wife. It got worse when he suffered a heart attack and had to work from home. Now I had to go to his house where I would be greeted by him answering the door in his silky robe. It was all so disgusting. I always prayed his wife would be home so I would not have to be alone with him. I remember being told, as he was going to be returning to work soon, that I would be required to put a nitroglycerin pill under his tongue if he suffered another attack at work! I think that might have been the lesser of two evils because another secretary had to clip her boss's fingernails. Gross!

I had not been in my position for even a year, but I was so unhappy. One day I called a couple of my secretarial instructors from SCC to get their opinion about quitting. They cautioned and encouraged me to hang in there for at least one year, saying that one year rather than six months would look better on my resume. How I wished I could quit, but I admired and respected my two instructors, so I hung in there, as they strongly recommended. As soon as my year was up, I bid out of his department. The utility promoted from within, so that was a relief.

Though I was young and new to the company, I had backbone and was not shy about speaking up. One of my responsibilities was to type up the testimonies of our officers who would be testifying in rate cases. Being a monopoly, for the most part, we could not just raise our rates. We had to justify them to a state body, the utilities and transportation commission, which decided our fate. Being nineteen, I realized I had much to learn. These documents were read by several in our company for accuracy. Well, a spelling error slipped through one time. Remember, I was transcribing this verbal testimony, some from written documents and some from transcription machines. In this case, the word was "eminent," and it was spelled that way in the document I was using. I remember double-checking the spelling because it was a word I was not familiar with. I did not know there was another similar word, "imminent." Whoever originally typed up the document used "eminent," which was the wrong word.

Our president at the time was a spelling, grammar and punctuation fanatic. He read all correspondence that came to him, usually getting caught up on his reading during weekends. He even used a red pen to point out errors. Well, the Monday morning following his red-pen frenzy, he wrote my boss a scathing note and attached it to the document with "eminent" circled in red. Knowing I would open my boss's mail and read the note that actually was intended for me, he unsparingly indicated his disgust about my ignorance. I still have a copy of that note. Basically it said that if my boss's secretary did not have a dictionary, buy her one!

I was horrified by "my" mistake and immediately apologized to my boss, indicating I did not know there were two similar words. I told him I was going to go speak with the president, take responsibility for the mistake and provide him some context. My boss begged me not to go down the hall to the president's office. I told him this was about my reputation and his, and I was going to set the record straight. To my dismay, his secretary would not let me see him. She indicated she would tell him, but I am pretty sure she did not. I was still relatively new to the company, and I did not want to have a bad reputation. I had no qualms about talking with the perturbed president, face-to-face. What rubbed me wrong was that the testimony had been read by several of the higher-ups, and none of them caught the mistake. This would not be the last time I rocked the boat by standing by my convictions.

I did have some fun times while in that first position. I got involved with the public relations department and participated in many functions and events the company put on for the employees. I was slowly becoming known throughout the company. My coworker, her roommate, (also a friend), and I became a singing trio and performed at the annual retirees' event. This event celebrated employees with at least twenty years of service. Honorees were treated to a wonderful evening of hors d'oeuvres, an elegant dinner, two adult beverages of choice and a delectable dessert, all provided by the company and held at Spokane's renowned historic hotel, The Davenport. One time the three of us sang with the accompaniment of Gonzaga University's prominent jazz band. The three-part harmony was really fun. We performed in long formal gowns that made me feel like a movie star. I loved performing.

This first encounter with a dreadful boss fueled my confidence to speak my truth. I was bold and stood up for myself early on. That was probably my biggest problem. I knew in my heart who I was at my core. I was not a "yes man" and also realized I had much to learn. I believed I deserved the same respect men were given.

When I was still in that first job, a senior electrical engineer sent a memo through the intracompany mail. Back then, all company memos were typed on a sheet of canary-yellow bond paper. Personal computers did not emerge until the '80s. A couple of engineers had purchased Apple MacIntosh personal computers, but the rest of the employees only had access to a mainframe computer with "dumb" terminals. Secretaries were still typing on typewriters; granted, they were fancy IBM Correcting Selectric typewriters. These wonders had both black typewriter ribbon and white correction tape that would remove misspelled letter(s) using a white sticky tape. It was great because at least on non-carbon copy paper memos, you could quickly correct a mistake and go on. If you had carbon paper in your typewriter, you still had to manually erase the mistake on each carbon copy, being careful not to drop eraser crumbs in between the carbon sheets, as those eraser marks showed up as squiggly dots on the subsequent copies.

Anyway, this senior engineer sent my female boss a technical memo. At that time, it was very unusual that a woman held a technical position. He was looking for her comments on something. He accidentally sent it to me, as she and I had the same first name, though she spelled hers differently than I did. Did I mention that on my first day of work, this woman told me I needed to pick a different first name so she and I would not be confused? Since my middle name is Jean, I went by PJ for the first year of my career. One of my SCC instructors called me at work one day and let me know that my perky, upbeat greeting of, "This is PJ!" sounded like I was a Barbie doll. Anyway, being respectful of this more experienced, seasoned engineer, I called him, wanting to let him know the memo inadvertently came to me and that I would pass it on to Pattie. His demeaning response was, "I will resend it. You wouldn't know anything about what I was talking about, because you are just a secretary!" That is all it took to get my hackles up, as this was another example of a male denigrating a female's skills and abilities and me wanting to, needing to, prove him wrong. I decided to talk with some of my engineer friends about what had occurred and if they could help me with a reply to him. Engineering and the department where I worked, were all on the same floor. Since my coworker's roommate worked in engineering, I got to know a few of the engineers through her.

I explained to these two engineers what the senior engineer had said, and I wanted him to know I did know something. Would they help me by reading the memo and providing the comments he was asking of Pattie? My plan was to memorize their words and practice delivering my informed comments to him in person. Remember, this happened all within the first nine months of my career. I could hardly pronounce kilowatt let alone easily type it or understand what it really meant. Even though I did not know anything about what this senior engineer was referring to, it did not stop me from proving his behavior ignorant of the changing times.

They were eager to help my cause. They thought the senior engineer was kind of pompous, and felt it would be amusing to be a part of putting him in his place. All the better that a new gal would take him on rather than the two of them! They provided me detailed comments, just enough to sound like I knew what I was talking about. I practiced in front of them a few times and they said, “You’re ready. Go get him!”

I walked down the hall to his office. He was there, sitting at his grand 1950s wood desk in a matching squeaky swivel chair. I was standing, which meant I was looking down at him. Anyway, he seemed bothered by me coming in. I told him I had read his memo that was inadvertently sent to me, and I had some ideas. “Would you like to hear them?” I innocently inquired.

A smug grin filled his face as he chuckled, “Yeah, I’d like to hear your thoughts.”

I quickly began reciting my memorized speech. As I was talking, he interrupted me and surprisingly said, “This is good. I need to write this down.” I got to the end of my speech and knew I needed to high-tail it out before he asked me any questions

I said, "Well, I need to get back to my desk," and quickly left his office. The two engineers who had prepped me were down the hall near the elevators anxiously waiting to hear what happened. They were sort of giddy! I proudly told them of my success, and they said they wished they could have been flies on the wall in order to see his face. Needless to say, that senior engineer treated me with more respect after that. My strongly-held belief that men thought women were "less-than" was boiling up inside me, lit by the garden incident, my unprofessional first boss and now this jerk. *This was definitely going to be an uphill battle*, I thought.

I tried to find balance among deference for my elders who were usually in positions of power and authority, with my belief that all people should be treated equal and with respect. Those ideals seemed to be characteristics at the opposite end of the company's cultural spectrum. This would not be the last time I spoke up for what I believed in.

When I finally bid out of that first department and got my second job at the utility, I became one of two secretaries in the marketing department. I went from the third floor to the first floor and from a four-person department to a department with more than thirty employees. I remember my desk and the other secretary's desk actually sat side-by-side, our metal desks touching. I quickly found out that she had bid on the job I had just been awarded and was very unhappy she did not get it. It was obvious she felt more qualified and deserving. My first day in that new role she stated, sarcastically, while puffing on her fourth cigarette, "If you think I'm going to train you, you've got something else coming!"

One of my mottos had always been "kill 'em with kindness," something my mom preached as I was growing up. It usually improved relationships, as long as it was authentic. I always looked for and found something to like in those who were sometimes hard to like. It was my goal to make sure this woman felt needed and important. In a short time, she became more friendly and helpful.

After about six months in marketing, another job in the department became vacant. It involved energy conservation (EC). I had interacted with the current EC representatives and did a ride-along with one. I was really interested in this job as a next step in furthering my career. I wanted to learn and experience more. I bid on it, but was unsuccessful. Even though I had secured the secretarial job I longed for, I believed there had to be more to jobs and work than this current position afforded me. I felt I had accomplished what I set out to do and now needed a new goal.

Marketing worked directly with operations (Ops), the construction side of the company. Ops was housed in a service building in the back of the campus. Later I came to know that the Ops field personnel, specifically electric linemen and natural gas servicemen, referred to the building I was working in as the Glass Palace. The Glass Palace was aptly named, as it was a five-story, glass-window structure where the executives resided and where administrative employees worked. Executives were referred to as "suits," as the service building employees were not enamored with anyone in the Glass Palace.

It was that second job in marketing, working with the field employees, where I fell in love with operations. It housed most of the blue-collar jobs, something I could relate to since my dad was a blue-collar sheet-metal mechanic.

I soon realized I preferred to work with men. Women seemed petty and picky and were always complaining and comparing themselves to each other. Men seemed to be more straightforward and candid. I always knew exactly where I stood with them in any given moment.

So, as I researched and reviewed the organizational chart, I decided on my career path and specific long-term goal, Vice President (VP) of Operations. I realized I needed to work myself up the ladder, and there was a specific ladder you needed to climb. I needed to get a technical job in operations, then a supervisory position there and then secure a leadership position working in one of the outlying construction offices. The path was pretty clear back then. I just needed to figure out how to maneuverer the twists, turns and speed bumps. Mentors were not a common resource back then, especially if you were a woman and had not been anointed by upper management. *I was a no-body*, I thought, and strongly believed I needed to prove myself to me and to everyone else, especially the men. Since operations was mostly comprised of men, I would continue my struggle, my fight, to prove my worth in this male-dominated company and department. As a secretary in marketing, I had to overcome the perceptions others already had of me. I was a competent secretary, and it was a challenge to loosen those perceptions when it came to me bidding on technical positions.

I strategized a plan on how to get some technical experience and skills. The company did not do job-sharing or much job-shadowing at the time. As I began to look for ways, a temporary job came open, supervising a new energy conservation program. The goal of the water heater wrap program was to conserve kilowatts (energy).

I bid on it and got it. Though I was in marketing, this job was my first leadership role associated with operations. I was twenty, almost twenty-one years old. I was in charge of about a dozen college students, many of whom were close to my age. The utility's current chairman of the board came to the company by way of that job; however, he was not part of the team for which I was responsible. A gentleman from outside the company was also hired into the same supervisory position, and we were to co-lead our teams.

This was 1981, and I hope you will appreciate the interview questions. At that time, there were no women leaders in operations. I was interviewed by white males, those who grew up in a work era before my time. I believed they saw me as a woman and a secretary, not possessing any technical skills or abilities. I distinctly remember answering the following question, "Two of your employees are physically fighting in the parking lot. What are you going to do about it?" Really? I wondered if they asked the male candidates that question. I confidently and rapidly responded that I would physically break up the fight, get them calmed down and find out what happened that got them to that point, as any logical person would do.

I remember the manager who let me know I was being awarded the job (promotion). His exact words, "Well I didn't think you'd make it, but the numbers came out differently, so I guess you get the job." Again, really? You can imagine how much this boss was going to be encouraging to my career. This was another notch in my belief belt that I needed to keep struggling and proving myself. It is easy for me to look back, in hindsight, and see how I let my early thoughts, feelings, and beliefs sway my perception of what was happening to women and specifically me. Where might I have been without that belief?

This manager and another manager in marketing felt similarly about a woman working in their world. The marketing manager remarked to me one day, when most of the guys were out of the office, "You realize you don't belong here. You belong at home. You are taking a position away from one a man should have." That was inspiring! How archaic this company seemed in light of the changing workplace demographics. Were they not aware of the Equal Rights Amendment that passed the U.S. Senate in 1972 and was sent to the states for ratification? To this twenty-year-old female, it seemed the company culture, or many of the men's words and actions, were lagging behind legislation aimed at the equal treatment of women in the workplace. Respectfully, I informed him I did not have anyone at home waiting for me or needing me. Sheesh!

I was a supervisor in the water-heater wrap program for about six months, until one more incident in this role left me fed up with this antiquated culture. The last straw was when I had a question regarding my paycheck and asked to see my co-worker's, the other supervisor's paycheck. We were hired on the same day, with the same job description. I had been with the company about one and a half years, and he was hired from the outside. I wrongly assumed that being a new position, we both were paid the same. To my surprise and disgust, he made more than I did! Why? We were doing the exact same job with exactly the same responsibilities and accountabilities. Finding out my lesser pay, I pushed the fact with my boss. Remember, this is the manager who already was not my biggest fan. He scoffed at my request, so I took my issue to Human Resources. They quickly acknowledged the error and gave me a pay raise. I now would be making 50 cents more a month, than him. I guess the company thought that would be a good incentive.

So, I quit! Other employees were shocked, because no one quits their dream company that provided a steady paycheck and was basically a monopoly. In fact, the president at the time, a staunch company-grown electrical engineer, saw me in the hall one morning before my last day. He was standing by the elevator waiting to go up to his office on the fifth floor. I was still located in the marketing department on the first floor. I was standing outside the glass doors of the department when he kind of hollered at me from down the hall, "I heard you quit my good company. Why?"

In no uncertain terms I defiantly retorted, "We are just one step up from government. We really don't have to provide good customer service, because where are our customers going to go? That's the customer-service mentality here. And another thing," I added, "You're still using "Dear Sir" in business letter salutations and there are women in the work world."

He was stunned to hear such an unabashed young employee defame the company he helped build. He was at a loss for words, which was not typical of him. He just responded, "Oh!" as the elevator door opened and he stepped in.

Can you see how the garden incident shaped how I saw every woman-versus-man incident going forward? I think I was too focused on proving my worth as a woman, rather than viewing myself as just an employee. With my belief and these interactions, I could only see the unequal treatment. Like focusing on a pothole in the road that you want to avoid but you hit it instead, my focus drew more similar situations and occurrences to me. I could not see nor experience something different than what I firmly believed. Was I experiencing unequal treatment? I would still answer yes, in some instances. However, my feelings and beliefs got reinforced, and focusing on the unequal treatment did not help my case.

I now know from experience that whatever I concentrate and focus on grows. The more I reinforce it, the easier it becomes to believe it. Multiple sites define belief in this general way: a belief is an acceptance that something is true. Therefore, all a belief is, is something I think about long enough, until I believe it. I was putting belief roadblocks up for myself and did not even know I was doing it. I chose to believe these behind-the-times old, white males were holding back every woman in our company who wanted to influence work through nontraditional roles. I often wondered how these men treated their wives and daughters.

I quit after working there for only two years. During this time, my mom had joined an American manufacturer and multi-level marketing distributor of natural nutrition supplements, weight-management and beauty products and a variety of household items. Her business had grown so large that she needed help managing it. She was like her dad, my Grandpa Nicol, who unfortunately died long before I was born. He could sell snow to a snowman, Mom would proudly reminisce. However, he did not like running the business, and he had created several businesses. He owned an ice house where he stored and sold ice, a roller-skating rink, a gas station and a theater. I think running the business was not as enjoyable to him as building it. Mom's passion was helping others. When she found something that helped and she believed in it, she felt everyone needed to know about it. She liked the one-on-one personal sharing. She personally sponsored over 300 people into her business.

I liked the secretarial and managerial aspects of her business, but I hated the selling part. I now am in the process of creating a jewelry line and am not yet comfortable selling my own designs. When my mom was alive, she would be my jewelry sales representative at the annual company Christmas crafts sale. Her natural love of sharing things and her belief in my talents made my jewelry marketable. I was too shy and somewhat embarrassed to tout my wares.

CHAPTER 7

I'M BACK!

Less than a month after I quit, one of the commercial/industrial marketing representatives I had worked for in that secretarial job in marketing, called me. He offered me a temporary job with a $400-per-month raise. With that incentive, I felt I could not turn him down. He later told me that was why he got the okay to offer me that amount. He wanted me to head up a streetlight research project, and he did not want me to say no. I really liked him. Even though he talked gruff and seemed aloof, he was a kind and considerate individual.

So, I came back to the company I had quit less than a month earlier and was back in the marketing department. I was project manager of a high-profile job of verifying the thousands of street lights in the city of Spokane. Throughout our company's history, the streetlight count had always been a bone of contention with this particular city. The city was accusing the company of overcharging them because our street light totals did not match their records. They were sure our company owed them money. My job was to rectify the streetlight records. I got to work with my favorite area of the company, Ops.

At about that same time, I decided to return to SCC to obtain a Liberal Arts degree, so I could transfer to Eastern Washington University (EWU) in Cheney, Washington, and earn a Bachelor of Arts degree in business. This decision affected the hours I could work, and my new boss was happy to oblige. I attended EWU in the morning and worked at the utility afternoons and evenings. Many times, I would be the last employee to leave, so I was required to shut down the computers that housed the streetlight data before leaving. This involved typing code in the mainframe computer for accomplishing this shutdown. I was not versed in the computer language being used, so I made sure to follow the instructions exactly as indicated.

As part of my streetlight data research and analysis, I also got to learn how to plot the correct x and y streetlight coordinates on the company's mylar distribution maps in the drafting department, housed in engineering. Until the company went digital a number of years ago, I would occasionally see my initials on those map copies. The streetlight project helped me develop some technical skills and demonstrated my technical ability. It is also where I met back up with that shy guy who delivered the mail at the community college.

He and I became inseparable. We would talk for hours over the phone every day. We would call each other first thing every morning, talk a bit before we headed to work, catch lunch together when we could, and see each other every night after work. We would laugh at our individual silliness and find joy and adventure in the simple things. I wish I had realized that our relationship was what I had been longing for, but I could not see it at the time. We supported each other in everything we did, and our families hoped we would remain together. I was not that smart, however. I thought love was what I saw on the Hallmark channel. I did not realize how special he was and that what I longed to have was right in front of me. Pushing him away was and still is the biggest regret of my life. I am thankful for his love and support and all the heart-felt memories. He has a part of my heart that belongs to him and him, alone. I take solace in my belief that everything happens for a reason.

I really enjoyed this streetlight project which took about ten months to complete. In the end, my research and analysis resulted in the city owing the company a large sum of money. The company decided to be a good community partner and did not request reimbursement. This information made our local newspaper, though my name was not mentioned. A few months ago, I found that newspaper article in a bin of scrapbook-worthy memorabilia. I am in the process of tossing much of this stuff out. Having no children, I have realized that when I pass on, someone from my family, maybe some nieces and nephews, will have the arduous job of sorting through all these only-understood-by-Patty bins. I can just imagine them wondering what the heck Aunty Patty was thinking, saving all this junk!

During this project I had the opportunity to work with different folks in operations, specifically what is referred to as the Line office on the Spokane Line dock. The word Line referred to the many electric linemen (those who construct and maintain transmission and/or distribution electric lines) who worked in the service building and had a dock where they parked and loaded/ unloaded their Line trucks. With these interactions and experiences, I was living my dream and climbing another rung on the ladder of one day becoming Vice President of Operations.

Other temporary jobs came up when I finished the streetlight project, which resulted in me being a temporary full-time employee for another year and a half. I even had the opportunity to work with two employees who each would later become President/ CEO during my tenure.

While in my secretarial job in marketing, I had a need to call the service dispatch group, who were also located in the service building adjacent to the Line dock. These dispatchers assisted me with many technical electric and natural gas questions I was being asked by customers who called in to get a new service, get a service moved or just had a question. One of the first questions I received was, "Why can birds sit on the electric lines and not get electrocuted and yet people can die by just touching one?" *Good question,* I thought. Of all the service dispatchers, there was one man and one woman who took extra time and provided me answers to all my questions. After taking time to go out to meet them in person and working with them frequently over the phone, we became friends. They helped me learn more about what all of the Line office employees did.

While still in my secretarial role in marketing and after learning more about operations, I needed a short-term strategy to get more exposure to and interaction with employees in the service building. Being an hourly employee meant I was entitled to two, fifteen-minute breaks daily and a sixty-minute lunch. So, I approached some of the women out there and asked if there was any way I could help during my breaks and lunch. They looked at me as if to say, "Seriously, you want to help in any way?" They quickly said I could file the E-size (34" x 44") blueprint maps that documented our electric and natural gas facilities. Blueprint paper is specially coated paper and is rarely used anymore. When the coated paper is exposed to the light, it turns blue. Blueprints were one of the first ways to make copies of plans or drawings. The field guys would pull out these maps to look up something, but hated putting them away. This resulted in a pile of maps that grew larger as the day progressed. The gals in the office were responsible to put all of them back in their specific drawers in numerical order and so it was deemed a menial job, one the women disliked. I offered to file them twice a day and sometimes on my lunch hour. They said, "Sure!"

I would file maps and sometimes, if one of the guys was not in too much of a hurry, I would ask him to explain what he was trying to determine. Sometimes a few even explained what some of the symbols meant. They were patient with me, and I think they liked that I was curious.

I was out there for about a week, filing maps at least twice a day, when one of the linemen asked me who I was and why I was there. I excitedly stated that I wanted to work in operations someday and this was affording me the opportunity to learn a little of the technical stuff. That seemed to suffice and was appreciated on some level.

After finishing the streetlight project, the other temporary jobs I had moved me around the company so I could no longer volunteer my services in the Line office. But while in my last temporary position, I was eligible to bid on and be awarded a permanent technical job in Ops natural gas distribution. I finally broke the secretarial ceiling and now held a technical position. I was thrilled! My long-term goal was slowly coming to fruition, one job at a time.

Even though I was in a technical job in operations in the service building and worked with the Line personnel, I was on the natural gas side of operations. As the natural gas employees used to complain, "Gas is the bastard stepchild of operations. The electric side gets whatever they want, and we get the leftovers." In other words, electricity was king. The natural gas guys were looked down upon. In some ways, it was a self-fulfilling prophecy, as the gas guys believed they were less-than and then acted as if it were true. I observed them jockey for position against the electric side, trying to be seen, heard and valued. I could relate to the natural gas employees, who felt less-than in the opinions of the electric employees. Bringing my "women are less than men" belief with me, I decided I needed to learn the electric side if I expected to advance in operations. All the while, I was taking every technical, supervisory and HR-related courses and trainings the company offered, in order to become more technically savvy.

The strategy of volunteering to file maps early on in my career, and in the process learn more, worked so well that I decided to try a similar strategy. We had an electric two-man night crew who worked from 4:00 p.m. until at least mid-night. The day shift ended at 3:30, Monday through Friday. None of the electric guys wanted to work the night shift, but there was plenty of work that occurred during the off-hours and having a night crew provided quicker service and saved the company money in reduced over-time. So, I asked if I could ride with that crew for one week to learn more about electric trouble after hours and how it was handled. This would not be allowed today, as safety rules have changed over the years, but I rode in the big Line trucks and sat on a bin between the driver and the rider. There was no seat belt because there was no seat! I had to hold on to their shoulders as they traversed corners and bumpy roads so as not to fall into either of their laps.

They got used to me asking lots of questions and always offering to help, no matter what the task. They started allowing me to help by letting me assist with a few very safe and menial tasks. I quickly graduated to cooler and not-so-safe tasks. They would take me up in the bucket of the Line truck. The rather small bucket snuggly fit two. They would allow me to do some of the work, like changing out a dead sun switch on a street light. That was a safety no-no back then, and it certainly is now! I loved feeling like I was part of their crew. A full crew is made up of a combination of a foreman, journeyman linemen, a groundman and sometimes an apprentice. The number of different classifications depends on the work to be done. Apprentices, who were usually the helpers, were routinely addressed with the slang term Grunt. In the office the electric general foreman for the overhead (versus underground) electric system knew I hated that term. He used to chuckle when he would be having trouble with the copier, and he would holler for his office Grunt to help him. That was me! I got a chuckle out of it, though, because he always treated me respectfully. He knew I liked the baseball caps with the company logo on them. These were a form of recognition of a job well done for the guys. He would always save one for me and hide it in his bottom desk drawer. He would wait until the end of the day to give me one, when most of the guys had gone home. He would make a big deal about the fact that he was giving me one, and I was not supposed to tell the guys where I got it. It was a fun game we played together.

My daily routine during this self-developed training week was to work my eight hours and at about 3:45 p.m., I would change out of my office clothes (I called them my nice clothes) and get into my work clothes. Working with the men in the field, I learned about layering my clothes so I could stay warm and still be able to move around. They were good to me. Each night I would document the day, time spent and what

I learned. It was this documentation that helped prove and improve my technical knowledge and demonstrated my initiative. I was also building relationships with these bargaining-unit employees and getting my hands dirty, literally—and doing it on my own time.

Later when I was bidding on my first operations management position, one of the electric foremen with whom I had ridden during those night ride-alongs made a statement in front of all the guys during an operations meeting at which I was in attendance. He said, "Patty likes to learn and is not afraid to admit not knowing something. She was willing to take her own time to learn and appreciate what we do, riding with us back then; I know she'll bring that same learning attitude with her to this job. I want that kind of person as my manager." My strongly held belief was getting a few holes poked in it. These men were willing to give me an equal shot to learn and grow and stand toe-to-toe with the men who were also bidding on the job. Backing me in that manner was definitely not the norm, and it was a show of faith in my abilities and in me as a potential operations leader.

During the time as the Natural Gas Technician, my first permanent operations position, I learned how to work with the craft personnel while still finding a way to be myself.

There were only a handful of women in the Line office, most in administrative roles. It was important for me to be "one of the guys" without being one of the guys. As I have mentioned before, I have a curvy figure and am sufficiently endowed. I always tried to dress so as not to accentuate this physical attribute, mostly by wearing blazers over my polo shirts. Every now and then, I would wear a dress that accentuated my entire figure. Several of the guys had a habit of staring at my chest, no matter what I wore. I got tired of it and decided to let them get their fill and hopefully get over that perceived obsession. One day I wore a powder- and navy-blue striped turtle neck sweater. Now my figure was there for all to see. I walked out onto the dock that morning before the crews left and hollered, "Take a look. Take a long look and get it out of your system!" I walked back into the office to laughter and even some cheering. You might think this was inappropriate, but after that my chest got fewer stares. Pretty bold of me, I know. I have many unusual stories from my years in Ops. I have been slapped on the butt, kissed on the job site for an apparent job well done and kissed in the office by one of my older employees, done in a similar manner to the iconic picture of V-J Day where a sailor was photographed kissing a girl in Times Square, New York City. I guess he thought he was being funny. Being a woman in a mostly male world came with its challenges.

I did not get that particular operations leadership position, so I kept searching for positions that would help me move up the path toward my ultimate goal. I wanted some HR background, so I bid on and was awarded a training coordinator position at one point. This slight detour off the operations/construction path provided me another opportunity to work with different areas of operations, building my relationship and knowledge bank. This experience would help me in the future.

At this point in my career, the only supervisory experience I had was the six months I spent leading the college students in the water-heater wrap program. It was about a year after my time in HR as a trainer, that I garnered what I viewed as my first big break. The then director of customer service, who would become the VP of Operations, had developed a leadership training program. He hand-selected a very limited number of employees to work for twelve months in various customer-service offices throughout our company's service territory. We would fill in for any manager who would go on vacation. This was a great leadership opportunity, especially because this director seemed to be on his way up. I never asked him why I was one of the few he selected. My perception was he wanted to mentor those he selected for future leadership opportunities. During that year, I filled in for three different managers, one in Spokane, one in southern Washington, and one in north central Idaho. As far as I could tell, he was pleased with my work and the employee and manager compliments. The feeling of being in his favor would be short-lived, however.

CHAPTER 8
LIVE AND LEARN

I knew I needed to get more supervisory experience. The water-heater wrap program was a nice start, but I was not in the position long enough and the opportunity was limited to a specific program supervising only college students. It did prove I could lead and manage teams and get bottom-line results, but I needed more.

There was a Customer Service Contact Center (call center) manager position in Lewiston, Idaho, that came open. I needed more supervisory experience, and it also checked the box of needing to work in an outlying office. I bid the job but got turned down. I remember talking with the call center director, the one who picked me for the leadership program. He wanted to know why I wanted to be a supervisor so badly. I confidently replied that research proved that people join a company because of the benefits or good things they have heard about the company, or comments from someone who works there. They leave, however, because of a direct boss. I believe leaders have the most influence on employees' productivity, their influence on bottom-line results and how much employees feel valued. I wanted to make a positive difference for employees and the company. His dry, but pointed reply: "Patty, you gotta learn to not rock the boat."

I replied, "If you're looking for a yes man, I'm not it. I will always voice my opinion, respectfully, and will do so until a decision is made. As long as that decision is morally and ethically solid, I will support it and not speak of my opinions thereafter. So, if you want a yes man, don't hire me."

Well, guess what? He did not hire me. I was in my late twenties or early thirties, and I believed my fate was sealed from that point forward. It was funny, because I had worked with this Director when we were both in marketing, many years earlier. He was assigned to our department to provide technical electric expertise to our marketing representatives. In my perception, his was knowledgeable and also a little quirky. He displayed characteristics of a typical engineer who believed these marketing representatives were too much fluff and not enough substance.

By the time this Call Center Manager position came open in one of our southern offices, it seemed his earlier, more positive view of me had changed. It might have been my yes-man comment, but actually I do not know. Maybe he perceived I had an ego. Maybe I challenged him in a way he disliked. Maybe I came across as a righteous feminist who believed she was his equal in terms of ability and maybe it had something to do with me being a woman without an engineering degree. Thinking back, I might have been carrying a woman-is-less-than insignia on my forehead!

I never regretted standing by my convictions with him that day. I knew my heart was in the right place and my leadership philosophy was on track. I continued to make a difference in the lives of work colleagues and my teams. That was more significant than a title. There is a fun twist to this story, which occurred a few years later. The man in that position was moved to another office. Guess who was hired then?

Still needing more leadership and technical electric experience, I looked at my career road map and decided a field engineer would be a good next step. These positions were mostly learned through on-the-job training. I had to bid on these open positions six different times before I was awarded one, but I would not give up. Each denial came with different requirements I needed to meet. Once I obtained the most recent changed criteria, they informed me that new criteria had been established and unfortunately, I did not possess them. This was the dance six different times. I found it ironic that one HR person, a woman who had been on five of the six interview panels for this job, was not on the panel when I finally achieved success in the sixth interview. I have experienced women who do not support other women succeeding. I believe that as women, we need to be advocates for all women, especially those who rise before us and/or those who rise above us.

Designing electric and natural gas jobs for residential, commercial and industrial customers required me to be in the field and on job sites daily. I dressed appropriately for an outside job, with nothing too body-shape revealing. One afternoon I came upon a commercial job and needed to talk with the foreman of the construction crew, not our employees. He and his crew just happened to be taking a break. As I approached them, they moved into a semi-circle to hear the conversation. The foreman had difficulty keeping his eyes on my eyes. He was basically talking to my chest. Feeling disrespected, I decided to give him a taste of his own medicine. Without missing a beat I squatted down, kept talking, staring directly at his crotch. His team went wild with laughter as they teased him that I got him good! After a minute or so, still without missing a beat, I stood up, kept talking and looked him straight in the eyes. He immediately focused his eyes on my eyes … point made! When I got back to the office, I told my boss he might be receiving a complaint and went on to explain what I had done. He laughed wildly and said, "I bet he doesn't do that again, without thinking!" In other words, what's good for the goose, is good for the gander.

I combined my persistence and belief with continuing to take advantage of any and all learning opportunities. I had no doubt I would eventually be a field engineer. This belief was just as strong as my opposite belief that I was being held back, by one individual, from my long-term goal of VP of Operations. Two strongly held beliefs both resulted in achieving exactly what I thought, felt and believed. Remember, when I continue to think a thought, it gets bigger. Mix strong feelings with those thoughts, and the result is a belief. With focus and effort, I have learned to tune into my thoughts and feelings. I want to be going toward what I want and not get stuck in where I currently am or have a negative belief that can hold me back.

Throughout my thirty-nine-year career, my mistake was believing I was being held back from my ultimate goal. On the flip side, I achieved every other goal along that path because that VP was not the immediate leader in any of those other jobs. Consequently, I had no resistance. I hope you understand the significance in the subtleties of unchecked beliefs. I held tight to my belief from the garden incident. I allowed a self-imposed limitation to result in a self-fulfilling prophecy.

Then in the mid-1990s, business process reengineering (BPR) became the latest business management strategy. The focus was on the analysis and design of workflows and core business processes. I became one of ten employees out of 1,400 to be selected by the executive team for a two-year role on our first and only reengineering (redesign) team. I felt a deep responsibility to represent all of our employees and felt privileged to do so. We were reengineering our core processes of serving our electric and natural gas customers. Throughout my career, I continued to be deeply involved in the company and got to know literally hundreds of employees throughout the four-state service territory. These relationships served the company and me. People were always commenting, "Patty knows everyone, and everyone knows Patty!"

I felt this selection would be a key role in my quest to be VP of Operations. I believed I was being seen in a broader light and so I kept learning and asking for and being given new and ever-challenging responsibilities.

About seven months into this two-year commitment, our company started a merger process with another utility. Our redesign team was disbanded, but many of the realigned processes were put into place. I was placed in an interim position reporting directly to the VP of Operations, which at the time was a woman. She had me checking in with the outlying offices to see if the realigned processes were being implemented. I remember one of the Line foreman in an outlying office thought my role was that of a snitch to corporate. On the Line dock one morning he aggressively confronted me in front of all the Line crews. As we stood toe-to-toe on the dock, he was standing so close his nose almost touched my nose and his spit was spraying on my face. He was turning red and getting angrier as his accusations got heated. I thought he would explode. As he accused and I adamantly explained that I had told all the employees, including him, what I was reporting to corporate, I remember thinking if he takes a swing at me, as a leader can I hit him back? My knees were shaking under my jeans, but I did not let him see my fear. As his voice got louder, everyone cleared out. It was just him and me, and I stood my ground. He finally turned around in disgust and kept loudly mumbling about me being a snitch as he stormed off. I stood there a moment, in case he turned back around, staring confidently at him. He did not turn around.

I was selected to take one of the realigned roles as Gas Operations Manager in an outlying office near the southern edge of our Idaho service territory. This was an important selection, because it covered two major criteria for moving up in operations. It was a direct leadership role with bargaining-unit employees, and it was in an outlying office. Bingo! I was feeling positive that I was on the path to achieving my career goal.

There is an interesting story on how I was welcomed into my new position. It was customary to have a going-away party for the leader who was moving to another position. In this case, there were three celebrations of leadership transitions, mine being one.

The party was held at a local pizzeria. Wives, husbands, family members, friends, and most of the employees were there to wish everyone well in their new responsibilities. When it came time to welcome me to the area and to my new role, there was a gift-wrapped box waiting for me. It was about eleven-by-seventeen inches and looked like it would hold a shirt. A few in the crowd hollered at me to open it up in front of everyone. There was no card, which made me a little nervous. I am blessed with being able to think on my feet and am usually not at a loss for words. This ability would prove crucial in my split-second reaction and what that said about who I was.

I unwrapped and opened that box, which contained a slightly smaller wrapped box. I could feel my heart picking up speed as I nervously chuckled, trying to seem amused. Upon unwrapping the second box, there was a third, much smaller box, which was also wrapped. Remember, I am standing in front of my new employees, most of the office team along with their family members, friends and my boss. As I unwrapped the tiny box, I saw printing on it. It said, "Summer Uniform." I felt my heart hit my stomach and a queasy feeling come over me, but I was still smiling. As I opened the box and unwrapped the tiny piece of tissue paper, it was an itty-bitty yellow bikini. I had only seconds to react.

In that brief moment, I realized my reaction would reveal if I could take a joke and to what extent. As I alluded to earlier, I have been endowed in the bust department. Though I always wore a jacket and rarely anything figure-revealing, it was obvious this tiny two-piece swimsuit was nowhere close to my size.

My quick wit raised lots of laughter when I vaguely inquired as I held it up to my chest, “Do you really think this is going to fit?” I sat down to the roar of applause, cheers and laughter.

Later I spoke with my boss who was in attendance that afternoon. He was not concerned with what had taken place. I said, “I didn’t know what to say, but knew whatever I said and how I reacted would set the stage for their first woman manager getting inducted into the linemen way.” My boss said I handled it perfectly.

That bikini is in one of my memorabilia bins and still brings a chuckle when I look at it, remembering the test I believed I passed with flying colors. I thought about making a miniature cutout of a body with a photo of my face on the head and pinning the bikini to it and placing it in my office on one of the filing cabinets. But I quickly smartened up, knowing it would only provoke more of the same.

I enjoyed being one of only two women leaders in operations at the time, among 1400 other employees, whose responsibilities covered these types of field personnel. They would test me in other ways, but much softer and with smiles indicating I was like one of the boys. I loved every minute working with and learning from them.

I did have a concern about being so far removed from the Glass Palace and the executive decision-makers. I had watched other managers go to an outer office, never to return to corporate. They were out of sight and out of mind. The female VP of Operations at the time knew my concern, and we discussed a return strategy. The only way back to headquarters was a management position in the call center, a job I had bid on earlier in my career. The twist to that earlier story was there was an abrupt change in leadership, and now I was being selected to take on an added challenge of managing two call centers, instead of one. This leadership opportunity required me to be in the office most of the time and allowed little interaction with electric and natural gas field personnel. I hated to leave operations, but realized it was my only way back, in the short term, to being closer to corporate headquarters in Spokane. Since I would be managing two call centers, one in north Idaho and the other in north central Idaho, I would be traveling back-and-forth every week. I was given the choice to live, north or north central, and I chose north. Between the operations job and the call center job, about four years passed until another opportunity presented itself.

CHAPTER 9

YOU'RE IT!

My next promotion was offered by a previous manager I had when I was a field engineer in Spokane. I liked working for him. He did not micro-manage, he allowed you room for trial-and-error and was there to support you through the learning. He liked to make work fun whenever possible.

He removed a manager who had responsibility for the electric and natural gas field engineers back in Spokane. He decided I was what the group needed to bring them together as a team, help individuals through performance management and build better relationships between field engineers and the bargaining-unit personnel. I found it interesting he is really the only one who believed my enthusiasm was just what the doctor ordered. In previous interviews I was often asked what I believed was one of my best qualities and many times my answer was my enthusiasm. With most men, this answer did not result in any brownie points. That did not matter to me, because employees positively responded to my energy. Early on, in operations positions, instead of signing memos with Patty, I signed them "P!" That became my trademark and still is today. Patty with an exclamation point!

A positive outlook, a can-do attitude and enthusiasm were my attributes. I know this mattered to those I served because they often mentioned that my positivity was contagious. That is still who I am at my core. I love helping others reach their goals while at the same time achieving the goals set before me by my leadership. My main reason for wanting to be VP of Operations was to have the ability to influence and serve at a broader level and help all those who had dreams to fulfill them.

During the two years I supported the field engineering team, I had more challenging opportunities from my male colleagues, and I had opportunities to poke fun at them as men. In one of our manager meetings the men, in my opinion, were being wishy-washy and not making a decision, something they usually did rather quickly but with not all the facts. This particular meeting was a continuation from the meeting before.

I decided to make my point by bringing visual aids. Are you familiar with Chinese cloisonne Baoding chiming balls that usually come in a brocade box? Baoding balls are metal balls small enough to hold in one hand. These Chinese therapy balls are designed to help relieve stress while building finger dexterity and wrist and forearm strength. Baoding balls are usually hollow and made from chrome-plated steel, with most containing a chime. People sometimes call these chime balls or harmony balls. I had purchased a set on one of my overseas adventures. I decided to bring them with me. As the men started in where they left off going back-and-forth and back-and-forth, I decided to "chime" in. I had the box hidden in my lap beneath the table top. I pulled out the box, placed it on the table in front of me, opened it up and said, "Gentlemen, here's my set. Where's yours?"

They roared and a few even turned a slight shade of red. One of them said, "Patty makes a good point. I'm ready to decide."

This somewhat gutsy move of not being afraid to play with the men served me well over the years. I gained respect, and they knew I did not take myself too seriously. Being a female in an almost all-male leadership role required walking a tight wire between not too girly and not a bitch. I felt I always had to be one step ahead of the men, prepared for anything.

My personality and leadership philosophy are to work hard and have fun. While being the manager of the two call centers, I had brought in a toy box filled with handheld electronic games, stress-relieving Dammit Dolls, small wooden paddles that had a rubber ball attached to the center by an elastic string and lots of Nerf guns that fired foam-dart ammo. The toy box was filled with these stress relievers. I took that box with me to this new role in operations. Who doesn't love a good Nerf gunfight?

One afternoon, most of the field engineers were in the office as it was nearing the end of the day. It seemed like a good time for all of us to let off some steam and have some fun. I announced with a yell across the office, to transfer their phones to their voicemail message boxes and pick a Nerf weapon from the toy box. The employees had high-wall cubicles, so that when they stood in their office, others could see a full head, tops of heads and/or fluffs of hair. With phones transferred, the fight was on!

Had one of our safety inspectors, my boss, or the president of the utility come in during that fight, I am sure I would have been severely reprimanded. I, and other daring employees, climbed onto the desk tops and peered over the sides to get better shots down into the cubicles. Several of us were running around the cubicles darting in and out, trying to find protection under desks. We were all laughing hysterically. I grabbed one of the fake potted plants and held it on my head. I ran down the cubicle corridors and if someone hit the plant with Nerf ammo, I would abruptly turn and go in the opposite direction, similar to those old carnival shooting galleries and arcade games.

After those of us older folks—I was about thirty-nine at the time—were almost out of breath because we could no longer laugh and fight at the same time, I shouted, "Truce!" Years after the fight, employees would reminisce about the fun they had that afternoon.

I worked in this capacity for almost two years when my boss decided to make another change in leadership. It was November of 1999, right before Y2K. As many will remember, there was an anticipated problem with the upcoming turn of the century, January 1, 2000. This problem was also known as the Y2K problem, the Millennium bug, Y2K bug, the Y2K glitch or as we referred to it, Y2K. The problem referred to the formatting and storage of calendar data for events beginning in the year 2000. Because many programs represented four-digit years with only the final two digits, the anticipated problem was the year 2000 would be indistinguishable from the year 1900. This could cause various errors in computer programs, such as the incorrect display of dates and the inaccurate ordering of automated dated records or real-time events. It was a world-wide worry without an easy remedy. On December 31, 1999, much of the world held its breath as the clocks clicked to an anticlimactic 12:00:01 on January 1, 2000. The world did not stop and time continued with no major glitches.

Prior to the 1999 Thanksgiving Day holiday, I had gone on an overseas vacation for almost four weeks. I returned home and back to work right after the holiday. Upon arriving at the office, one of my construction manager colleagues inquired, “Has the boss talked to you, yet?”

I said, “No, why?”

He replied, “You got a new job while you were on vacation.”

“What job?” I inquired. Once again my boss had removed that same manager he removed before from his current job and appointed me as his replacement. Only I was not excited to get this job. It was Emergency Services (Central Dispatch) Manager and the employees worked 12-hour rotating shifts making sure field personnel were available 24/7, 365 days a year to respond to electric and natural gas emergencies. That meant, as the manager, I would always be on call when there were emergencies in which I was required to assist my team in the restoration process. The bad news is that these emergencies happened frequently.

I teased my boss that I would think twice before going on another vacation overseas. He reminded me that the last time he moved me into a challenging role, he believed my new employees needed my enthusiasm and my ability to take a difficult group and bring them together as a team. He felt I could develop the new central dispatching process, which was in heated debate across the entire service territory, weed out any nonperformers, and at the same time develop those who were developing themselves. He said it was similar this time and based on my past success, he needed big things out of me once again. The upside to this job, was it was high-profile due to the need to return service to our customers quickly, safely and most efficiently.

I have always loved finding out about employees, who they are, what makes them tick and how I can assist them. I also am candid with them on how they can improve. I can deliver the tough stuff and do not shy away from it. I think it was because I spent a major part of my career being raised by linemen. They had a quick and frank way of delivering bad news, many times using colorful language to make sure you knew exactly what you did wrong. They would teach you to do it right or better. They then moved on, not holding that over your head unless you made the same mistake again. With this upbringing, I developed a thicker skin for receiving critical feedback. Though I have softened the colorful language, I still prefer to be candid when dealing with conflict.

In this new role, I had an employee who was very critical of me and how I led. One day in her performance review she said, "I want your job because I think I can do it better than you!"

I said, "Great! I just need to help you do it in a way that does not feel like your finger is poking me in the chest!" She was talented and had a similar desire to accomplish more and do it better.

I believe in supporting employees who go to bat for themselves, asking for feedback and input, taking advice and acting on it, working extra and doing what it takes to help others reach their goals. I also believe leaders should be so good at developing their employees that those employees may advance above them or before them. That is a legacy worth leaving.

My motto is, "The elephant in the room! I help solve that." I became comfortable with this lineman-approach to getting tough issues out on the table and getting them resolved. The frankness is only uncomfortable in the moment. As a leader, I like to move quickly to what I need to know in order to avoid making a mistake and learning how I can do better in the future. This straightforward approach to resolving conflict has been invaluable in my career. Combining this approach with listening, observing and asking questions always improved interpersonal relationships. I also have been aided by my sensibility and intuition to read between the lines in order to fill in the story of the person who may not be telling me everything verbally, but is expressing feelings through nonverbal communication.

I, too, am human and can let my feelings get hurt, but it never lasts long. I realize it probably is a learning moment in my life's journey, so learn from it and move on. I am a student of life and freely share my mistakes so others may learn from them.

CHAPTER 10

FALL FROM GRACE

As you can probably surmise, I had an interesting career: sixteen different jobs in twelve different departments. Many positions I raised my hand for and several I was recruited for and then placed in them. As long as I was not in the direct hierarchy of the VP of Operations who I believed had it out for me, my career looked like it was on an upward trajectory, not steep but still moving upward.

I was the Manager in Emergency Services (Central Dispatch) for almost six years. My direct boss was the same manager I had when I was the manager in operations in that southern outside office. The VP of Operations was his boss. The VP continued to make my boss's life harder, by continuing to find fault with my work. One day my boss approached me. He said, "Patty, I'm tired of fighting the VP and standing up on your behalf. It is exhausting. You are now on your own." I appreciated his honesty and understood what he had been going through. I became acutely aware that I was starting a major fall from grace.

I believe in being aware of the signs of change. Face the change, gather facts, analyze and determine the next steps. Since I realized I would not be supported in my goals in my current operations role, it was in the employees' best interest and the company's best interest for me to move on. My hope for the team was that their next leader would be supported by the VP. Consequently, after six years, I left operations for the last time and was no longer under the chain of command of the VP of Operations. About nine months after leaving, the VP was questioning the new leader about the budget overruns. She was directed to review my old budgets and provide justification for the additional expenses because there were no major changes since my tenure.

I was recruited by a wonderful woman who would become my boss until her retirement about five years later. She wanted me to take a role in her department—Business & Public Affairs—that would encompass being responsible for the greater Spokane service territory. It was 2005, and I was enjoying my new role. I was able to continue to work with and assist operations and use my technical experience in negotiating our company's various municipal franchise agreements. I also got to assist in economic development, workforce education and political issues affecting the future of our company. There were four of us throughout the company with the same responsibilities.

After a couple of years in this role, two of my counterparts were retiring, one in north central Idaho and one in north Idaho. Both wanted me to take their positions. Both thought I would be a good fit since I had worked in both communities in prior roles. The stipulation had always been, you had to live in or near the community you represented. My folks were getting older and my mom's health was diminishing, so I was not interested in the north central Idaho position since it was about 115 miles south of Spokane and about two hours and fifteen minutes away.

Our company president asked my boss if I would take the other opening in north Idaho. With the construction of my new home having just been completed, along with my mom's failing health, I told them both no. That was the first time in my career that I said "no" to a position the company wanted me to take. I remember my boss cautioning me that this could impact any further advancement in my career. I was okay with that. I had moved once before for the company. Living close to my aging parents in order to assist them was more important than advancing.

To my surprise, the president came back to my boss and asked, "Would Patty take the job if we did not make her move?" My boss posed that question to me. To my knowledge, this was unprecedented in the company's history. The president's action made me feel valued. He trusted me to figure out a way to be involved in the community in the right ways and that not living there would not be a problem.

I remember my response to my boss was "Yes, but it is gonna cost ya." Prior to that day, I dreamed of making six figures. For years it seemed like it was out of reach. I kept focusing on making that dream a reality, though I did not know how it would materialize.

In 2007 with this ask from my boss and the president, I decided I was going to realize that dream. I believe in visualization and being grateful for something I want, as if it has already manifested. For about nine months prior to getting this promotion, each day on my drive to work I visualized being given that raise. I could see all those zeros before the decimal point and felt the exhilaration of realizing that goal. I visualized from a place of abundance, allowance and nonresistance. I asked and then believed it would come. The more I visualized, the more I felt the excitement of the raise and the more real it felt. This repetitive thought, combined with strong positive emotions, turned into a belief. That belief turned into a reality.

I strive to be the person employees need. Another ritual on my drive to work is thanking God or the Universe for the plethora of things I am grateful for in my life. Then I ask for divine inspiration to be a good listener, or a co-solver of problems or be aware of the need to express a kind word or a thank you.

That day I told my boss it would cost her, the reality played out just like I had been visualizing it. As I look back on my career, I accomplished so much by believing I could. Yet I let one belief hold me back from my ultimate goal. I wish I could have realized that dichotomy earlier. But as I also believe, everything turns out as it should.

Whenever I have dreamed of something I think is big and above the norm of where I am currently at, it seems unattainable, in that first wish or ask. Consequently, in the beginning there is no feeling of belief that it will happen. That is why I immediately focus my thoughts on the feeling of it already being realized. The more I focus on those positive thoughts, the stronger my belief becomes and the more real the dream is. The more real it feels, the more confident I become in that belief. I only have control over myself, and I choose to believe there is abundance in the world and abundance for me and my dreams. I do not get everything I am dreaming of and hoping for. Sometimes I cannot let go of the desperate pleading I feel inside, which is actually me asking from a place of not believing it will happen.

I have proof of believing something wonderful will happen and believing the opposite, that something is unattainable. I do a decent job of manifesting what I want in my professional life, especially since I have transitioned from my thirty-nine-year utility career into my consulting business. Things seem to manifest much more quickly and effortlessly. I am sure one reason is because I have let go of the belief of someone holding me back from realizing my dreams.

My fall from grace got steeper and quicker when the VP of Operations became my boss's boss. He began inserting himself and his opinions into my performance reviews and career aspirations and started to tie the hands of my boss. At one review, my boss apologized for needing to revise my review and remove my aspiration of improving women's chances to succeed in operations. Later, my idea would be implemented by the VP through a different female leader. The good news, the idea got implemented and today women are rising in more technical areas of the company. It was hard for me not to be resentful that I was not being allowed to be innovative and to thrive. I let the fall-from-grace belief tumble my dreams and stifle my actions. Even though the reins got tighter for my boss, she still found ways to covertly assist me. She helped me be my best self through my current roles and responsibilities in the communities and with the companies and municipalities I served.

Just when I felt I was beginning to hit my stride again, in spite of who I believed was holding me back, my boss retired and the VP of Operations became my immediate boss. A sinking feeling came over me, as my worst nightmare became my reality. I unconsciously adhered to the feelings, thoughts and beliefs from the garden incident that occurred more than forty years earlier. I allowed my belief to get reinforced through the words and actions of those in power. I gave away my control of me.

I became paranoid and almost petrified in every conversation or interaction with him. Immediately, I was back to the belief he was still out to get me. My belief played out like a movie you have seen numerous times. The results could not be different from what I believed. I believed I could not do anything right and that self-fulfilling prophecy became my reality. Because I believed it, then acted as if, that belief played out right up to the day when my sage friend, Michele, asked me that one question, "Patty, could it have been that your belief he was holding you back, was what actually was holding you back?" Though that question was posed over two years ago, thinking about it still humbles me. It feels good to let go of that poor-me shield of armor. What I did not take into account back then, was the part I played in the path of my life. I was in charge; he was not. I allowed him to take charge by giving away my power to a belief I created.

When it came time for my first performance review with him as my boss, I asked him how much time he had allotted to talk with me. He said he had all the time I needed. When we sat down, the first thing I said was, "I have been under the impression you hate my guts. I have felt this way for over twenty years."

He seemed a little taken back by my candor. He kind of fumbled his words and replied, "Well, that is your perception."

To which I quickly replied, "Yes and my perception is reality to me." He then spent the next ninety minutes brainstorming the possibilities of finding a project for me that would assist in my pursuit of more operations experience. *An interesting response,* I thought.

There is so much more to the story of what he said about me to others and conversely how other leaders supported me through my career. What I hope I am conveying and ask you to consider is this: what do you believe about yourself, your talents, your weaknesses and what others think about you? When we believe something is fact, it can be difficult to start believing otherwise.

Over my sixty years when I have gotten a thought stuck in my head and have strong feelings or emotions around it, it is easy to believe it. I have asked the Universe, on more than one occasion, that if I am missing the obvious-to-others signs, to feel free to hit me over the head with a two-by-four to get my attention. Sometimes I have been slow to see the signs. And the question Michele asked me was that two-by-four. Thank goodness God uses the appropriate people at the appropriate time to get my attention. This helps me move toward what I want, instead of moving in the direction of what I do not want.

CHAPTER 11

BLESSINGS AND BELIEFS

Ever since the day I was posed that question, I cannot get the significance of it out of my head. What if that realization was true? Thinking about my answer catapulted me into taking back control of my life. It is so annoying to learn something the hard way. I can be so stubborn and thick-headed sometimes. Instead of looking at situations that are not working and looking for a different approach, I do the same thing over and over, expecting different results! What I believed was what I was experiencing. I gave my power away, instead of taking my power back and questioning my own behavior and analyzing the results. Again, I just tried harder instead of trying something different.

Upon pondering that ominous question, my life was changed, never to return to the same thoughts and resentments I had been carrying around for more than thirty-nine years. I do believe I am exactly where I am today because of all the experiences in my life. I would not go back and change aspects of my professional life. Focusing on the past and the what-ifs is a waste of precious energy. Focusing on where I want to go and pre-paving what I want in life has beneficial results.

Per the sage advice of my sister, Jan, I started to look at each situation and issue that would arise and ponder what part I was playing in the outcome. I turned up the volume of the thoughts playing in my head, so I would not miss what was going on there. It was as if I could start and stop the feelings I was experiencing each day by paying attention to my thoughts and being aware of my emotions. I would immediately question why I was feeling a certain way. This was so freeing. It allowed me to take my control back. It was my life and now I was not willing to unconsciously give that control away to anyone. I was going to be present in my own life and catch myself living on remote control.

It should not be surprising how much more enjoyable each day has become. Even when the day is not stellar, I still feel like I am riding on top of the wave instead of being tumbled by the undertow.

When I think back on my career, I originally thought my fall from grace was solely related to my working relationship with the VP of Operations. What I now believe is that it was related to the garden incident experience and manifested into a strongly held belief. From there and throughout my working career at the utility, I unconsciously looked for things and instances that reinforced that belief.

As part of my last position with the company, I got involved in Rotary International at the urging of my predecessor. Rotary has been a wonderful opportunity to reinforce meaning for my life's work, "Service Above Self." It is rewarding to look to the needs of others, rather than focusing on my needs. I seem to do everything in extremes, all or nothing, so I remind myself that balance in all things is a meaningful goal.

I believe it is important to know who I am. The way I define that is to keep asking myself that question. I know I will stand up for what I believe is right. I used to take some pleasure in being right, which usually meant someone else was wrong, and my ego was leading. I have learned I do not need to make anyone wrong. I now try to tune in to my inner guidance.

This is a wonderful intention. However, I am quickly reminded of my dad teasing me in my adult life about my seeming to be like two people; one person in my work life and another person in my personal life. He would say, "I do not understand how you can be so successful in your work life and not apply those successful aspects in your personal life. When will you get tired of swimming upstream?" For some reason, I have put more effort into improving my professional life. Maybe I have spent more time building my career than building a solid personal life. For my entire career, my work defined me. Now my work is still an important part of me, but does not define me.

Life continues to unfold, with some blessings disguised as problems or challenges. Each day I start with thanking God for all my blessings, those I realize, those I take for granted and those that are disguised. I still feel immense guilt when I compare my life to many I come in contact with. I feel the need to give away what I have been so blessed to have.

Several years ago, one blessing came very disguised. Reflecting back to when I was using internet dating sites, I met a gentleman whose behavior seemed odd. He was quiet and seemed to have had a few hard knocks in his life. The genuine kindness I felt in his presence had me wanting to help him. We saw each other casually for a couple of months. One morning he stopped by my house to pick me up for breakfast. After I finished getting ready, I came out to the living room. I was shocked to find him lying on the floor, almost nonresponsive. I immediately called 911. As the paramedics were checking him, they pointed to a large scar down his chest that wrapped around to the upper part of his back. He was not fully conscious, so they asked me if I knew anything about it. It was the first time I had seen it, so I was no help. Having seen similar scars on other patients, they surmised this episode was probably related to it. Later that day in the hospital emergency room, I found out from one of his daughters that he had lung cancer and it had metastasized to his brain. He had been having brain surgeries for the past year and was living with his oldest daughter's family in a town about two hours north of Spokane. She let me know he would now need to return to his doctor and probably need to schedule his next surgery.

I felt bad for his family who would need to drive him to and from these appointments and then take care of him, after the surgery. My self-imposed guilt got the best of me, and I offered to let him stay with me, since I lived only miles from the hospital and his doctors. This inconvenience was the most extraordinary blessing. He stayed with me for several months, and I was at his bedside when he had the next brain surgery. What I learned during this time helped explain his odd behavior.

He was the gift, the blessing in disguise. He also gave me the most precious gift, a book that continues to positively influence my life, *Ask, and It is Given* by Abraham-Hicks (Esther and Jerry Hicks). He firmly believed the message in that book, that our thoughts and beliefs rule our life.

Four years earlier, he and his brother-in-law both got diagnosed with stage-four lung cancer at the same time. They both were given four months to live, however they approached their fate much differently.

He decided he was not going to die from it. He just decided. He asked God to live and believed it was given, and he lived his life that way. He would go to his checkups and did what the doctors suggested. He would survive surgery after surgery and always had a positive outlook. I remember that one time I was with him in the hospital. The nurses and doctors were hugging him, exclaiming they were so happy to see him, because by all accounts he should have died. That made an impression on me; he made an impression on me. I still have that book he gave me. His heartfelt words, his belief in good outcomes and his positive actions were living proof of the power of our beliefs.

Conversely his brother-in-law, with the same diagnosis, led an opposite life. Every day he talked about his diagnosis and was lamenting he would soon die. He was giving up and giving in. My friend told me he would desperately try to talk some sense into him, but to no avail. Almost four months to the day, his brother-in-law died. Powerful! My friend was a living example of what I would have labeled in the past as positive thinking. I think it was more than that; it was positive believing.

My mom believed in the power of positive thinking. She used to say things like, "This too shall pass. It won't always be like this, and the sun will come up again tomorrow and things will look better in the daylight." She was positive, maybe to a fault. She looked at life through rose-colored glasses, all of the time. When I was in a bad mood, sometimes her positivity was just annoying. I often recognize Mom's positive outlook in me—and probably some of that annoying characteristic, also. She would always see the positive in something and forced us kids to do the same. Because it was part of our upbringing and I loved my mom, I believed her and then usually acted "as-if." Most of my life I have been called "Sunshine" by young and old in both professional and personal settings. I am bright-eyed and bushy-tailed and have enough energy for a room of people. Sometimes this can be overwhelming; I have been told I am incorrigible.

I am positive and upbeat most of the time probably because it is who I am, and I like how that makes me feel. I like being the light in a room. Most people are not like me, and I am good with that. I feel so blessed that I want to share goodness and positivity with others. I believe many people have a much harder life than I do. I believe it is my responsibility to not focus on my little woes but rather focus on being positive and uplifting for them. I love to laugh and share my funny, self-deprecating sense of humor by telling on myself. This usually results in putting others at ease.

I love asking folks how they are or how their day is going, because I truly want to know the answer. There are some grocery clerks who seem surprised that I really want to know. When someone asks me how I am, I usually reply, “Great!” That gets the attention of most people.

Then I energetically ask, “How is your day going?” I try to find something to compliment them about and always thank them.

My daily focus is helping others in whatever way I can. I like bringing a little joy into their day. It is all about helping them see their value and helping them realize they can accomplish anything. There is nothing more satisfying. I am not responsible, however, for any positive change they choose to enact. They are the ones doing the work. My hope is that when they strongly believe in themselves and experience success, that feeling will spread into other things they want in their life.

Many have been conditioned to, "I need to see it, before I believe it." Because I am a life-long learner, I am constantly researching, reading and watching TED Talks and the like and find value in studying why people are successful. I believe a big part of their success is their passion for what they are doing and a deep, strong, unshakable belief that whatever they are striving for will come to fruition. They keep what they want in front of them, and they do not allow their focus to waver on what they have no control over. They keep their eyes on the prize no matter what. They do not listen to the nay-sayers and they keep forging ahead, because in their mind's eye it is already accomplished. They have already achieved their dream.

Years ago I read an article about how Olympians use their thought processes to aid their training. The one that still sticks with me was reading about Flo Jo,

Florence Joyner, in the 80's. She impressed me because she was only four months younger than I at the height of her success. She was an international track-and-field star and was known for her record-setting sprints in the 100m and 200m, as well as for her flamboyant personal style. She spent a great deal of time practicing her sprint in her mind. She even visualized the finish-line clock with the exact minutes and seconds of her winning run. She ran that race in her mind, over and over. She believed it, she felt it, and then she did it. Her finish time was exactly as she had visualized it. The world records she set in 1988 in the 100m and 200m have not been broken. *Florence Griffith Joyner. (2020). Retrieved September 30, 2020, from https://en.wikipedia.org/wiki/Florence_Griffith_Joyner.*

I also remember reading a *Reader's Digest* article about the power of our thoughts and mental rehearsal. I would add to that, the power of our beliefs. Researchers conducted a study with three groups of basketball athletes who were tested making free throws at the beginning of the experiment. One group practiced free throws every day for an hour. The second group just visualized themselves making free throws, and the third group did nothing.

After about thirty days, they brought the three groups back together to physically shoot free throws. The group that practiced in their minds improved slightly better than the group that physically practiced. The group that did not practice, saw no improvement. I remember hearing that Tiger Woods and Michael Jordan visualized success before they took a shot.

Why did the practice-in-their-heads group do so well? One reason: it is easier to perform perfectly in your mind. In this case, that group hit the basket each time. The group physically shooting would miss sometimes, requiring them to correct their mistake in order to improve. Positive and specific visualization makes a positive difference in real-world outcomes.

I had a similar experience in junior college. It occurred in my first year of taking executive secretarial courses. There was a course called "Shorthand." Shorthand, also called stenography, is a system for rapid writing that uses symbols or abbreviations for letters, words or phrases. The system popular at the time was Gregg. Shorthand was useful for taking dictation of memos and letters; it was something secretarial students were required to take in the late 1970s. I still use some shorthand today when I am taking notes in meetings or at workshops.

One day our Shorthand instructor was ill and the department chair filled in. I remember thinking, *how is he going to teach our class,* because I assumed he did not know how to take shorthand. In this class we would perform several practice tests, before the final timed test, where the instructor would read a memo or letter to us, and we would record it in shorthand. The pressure was on to keep improving your correct words-per-minute score. Instead of doing the regular practice tests as we normally did, he said he wanted to try something different. He proceeded by instructing us to, "Take out your finger." What? He must have meant take out your pen, right? Nope, he said it again, "Take out your finger and get ready to write!" Though we thought he had lost his marbles, we were curious as to where this was going. We completed all of our practice tests with just our index finger invisibly recording on our writing tablets. We did several of those practices.

Then he said, "Okay, take out your pen and get ready to write." I remember not feeling as anxious as I normally felt when the instructor would say that. This time, I was slightly anxious, but really curious. He then dictated a business letter that we had not heard before, and this was our timed test to be graded. We feverishly wrote with the ink sliding across the page. I know I had no idea how I was doing. It seemed I was writing all the words correctly, but not until we transcribed our notes would we know how well we did.

To everyone's surprise and delight, we each increased our dictation speed and accuracy. We were buzzing with excitement and questioning him as to why that was. He explained that when writing with your finger, like visualizing in your mind, you rarely make a mistake, because you cannot see your mistake on the page. You do not get frustrated and worried, which usually results in missing the next words dictated. For the most part, you think you copied down every word correctly because you cannot see anything different. It reinforced in our minds, and in our hands and fingers, that we were succeeding. I will never forget that class.

So, I ask you again. What do you believe and how do you feel about yourself, your life and your future? What do you believe is true about your abilities and talents? What do you believe about your future, personal and professional? What about your dreams and goals, your happiness?

Whatever you believe, IS! Beliefs come with strong emotions. Being more aware of your emotions, your feelings, will help you decipher your beliefs. It is your life, so why not be in control of the outcome? Why not get everything you dream of? There is plenty to go around, because I believe we live in a world of abundance. I know this is true, otherwise there would not be so many brands of toothpaste, laundry detergent, running shoes and golf clubs, to name a few.

Think of all the entrepreneurs in the world. How can so many of them be successful when there are so many others in the same line of business? Many of them are successful, in spite of the competition. There is abundance, if we believe there is. There also is scarcity, if we believe there is. I believe that a consistent trait successful people possess is their unshakable belief they will succeed. They believe in themselves, no matter how many nay-sayers there are.

I come back to the question Michele asked me. I was not ready to ponder the answer the first time she asked me if I wanted to explore that question. I was adamantly opposed to going down that path. I dug in my heels and wondered why she seemed to know something I did not. Our beliefs are our life. It is for us to believe or not believe, to act or not act. We can blame others for our belief they made us do it or made us feel a certain way. When we believe that, who is in control? Not us, but them.

Pearls of wisdom are always available, and that is why I still like to read self-improvement books. There is a story in Jack Canfield's and Mark Victor Hansen's *Chicken Soup for the Soul* book. From memory it goes something like this: If a random stranger comes up to you and says your hair is green, you sluff it off; you do not believe this person because you know your hair is not green. However, the passage goes on to say, if someone you trust and respect tells you something you may not be aware of or are unsure of, you may tend to believe him/her. Do you question it from your belief or do you just take what he/she has said as truth, as a belief?

I saw this kind of belief behavior occur many times. A colleague of mine had two daughters. The youngest was about ten. She was kind of clumsy and fell down quite a bit. When I first saw her trip, I thought, *oops.* Then I heard her dad, my school colleague, emphatically state, "You are so clumsy; you are always falling down!" He uttered similar comments every time she stumbled or fell. Being only ten, she probably believed her dad. Every time she demonstrated being clumsy and her dad reinforced it, she was, in fact, clumsy. This then seemed to be the truth. What if she chose not to believe her dad? What if she had ignored her dad's comments? If her thoughts, feelings and beliefs were not of being clumsy and falling down, there is no way she would have been. What you believe, IS! What you feel and your emotions around your beliefs are your indicator.

I reinforced to myself that the VP of Operations had it out for me, and that he was holding me back. By focusing on that, constantly having my radar up and looking for confirmation, telling others about it and having others report to me when they heard him talk negatively about me, I was doing everything to reinforce my beliefs through what I saw and experienced. If I had focused on what I wanted instead of what was playing out in front of me, things might have turned out differently.

I used to believe I was a great multi-tasker. Recently I heard a speaker provide a definition of multi-tasking and examples of the difficulty of performing multiple tasks at the same time. His premise was that most people are better at focusing on one thing at a time. For example, I cannot accurately follow two different cooking recipes at exactly the same time. When I am looking at what ingredient to put in next for one recipe, I physically cannot have that same focus on the other recipe at the exact same time. I cannot focus on what

I want when I am focused on what is playing out in front of me. It has taken practice to look away from what is, when what is, is not what I want. It is much easier to be captivated by what is happening in the moment. From experience I have learned that whatever I concentrate and focus on, gets bigger. What I mean by that is remembering what it was like learning to ride a bicycle. I first learned to ride a tricycle, which was easy and I felt safe. Learning to ride a taller, two-wheel bike was kind of scary. Back then, the bicycle tires were big and fat which made it difficult for me to maneuver in our dirt alley. Our one bike had only one gear, the rider peddling it. I remember Dad holding the back of my bike seat as I was first learning how to ride it. Dad would be running alongside me holding the back of the seat as I pedaled the bike. Knowing at some point he would let go, I would plead, "Don't let go Dad, okay? Don't let go!" I realized he had let go when I no longer heard him encouraging me. I remember falling the first time I assumed he let go when his voice became faint. I was so mad at him for betraying my trust by letting go. It did not help that he would chuckle when telling me we all fall when we are learning. The two things I remember most about the alley were all the potholes and bumps, frightening for a first-time rider. I remember fixating on a pothole and chanting to myself, “Don’t hit it, don’t hit it!” What do you think happened? Yup, I hit it. Why? Even though I thought I was focused on not hitting it, my focus was on the pothole. My eyes were fixated on it. There is no way I could have missed hitting it. In other words, I brought the hole to me on my bike. Whatever we focus on gets bigger and if we keep focusing on it and replaying it in our minds, our thoughts and words we say about it become a belief and that belief becomes reality.

CHAPTER 12

MANIFESTATIONS

I had an unforgettable event in my life when my belief about becoming a private pilot resulted in disaster and success. For some reason—I still do not know where I got this thought—I just knew I was going to crash a plane at some point. This was in my head from the very beginning of my taking flying lessons. I was scared every time I went up, wondering if this would be the time I would crash. I believed it was just a matter of when, not if. I had those same thoughts every time I even thought about flying and especially when I was flying without my instructor.

I focused on this belief until it got so big, it became real. It was my last required flying maneuver before I would take an oral exam and then the practical exam or checkride. I had already successfully passed the required written exam. It was a snowy Sunday morning in December, 2007. We had record snow in Spokane and surrounding areas, specifically in north Idaho, where I would start my last requirement of my private pilot training, a long cross-country flight. This required flight has to be at least 150 nautical miles total distance, with full-stop landings at three points, and one segment of the flight consisting of a straight-line distance of more than fifty nautical miles between the takeoff and landing. The day before, the snow kept falling and the warm sun shined brightly slightly melting the top layer. The runway had been plowed, which meant that slightly melted snow became a two-foot cement-like berm on both sides of the runway. That bright winter sun had also left the runway like an ice-skating rink. I started at my home airport in north Idaho which is about thirty miles south of British Columbia, Canada. I would be flying from the Canadian border approximately 191 nautical miles south to north central Idaho.

Because of the multiple airports I would be flying to that day, my instructor and I decided a very early morning start would be best. I remember that cold Sunday morning. The airport apron (the area of an airport where aircraft are parked, unloaded or loaded, refueled, or boarded) where my plane sat, was extremely icy. My instructor and I had a hard time remaining upright while fueling the plane. She even walked out onto the runway and came back and warned me to be very careful. "Do not overuse the rudders and definitely do not use the brakes," she cautioned me. She went inside the office while I finished fueling the plane. Two experienced pilots pulled up on the other side of the fueling tanks and fueled their plane. We chatted, and they took off. My instructor called them on the radio and inquired about the condition of the runway.

The co-pilot quickly replied, "It's slicker than snot!"

With that, my instructor warned me again, "Be very careful, okay?" She must have believed in my flying abilities to send me that day. I later found out that the two seasoned pilots had no idea I was not an experienced pilot. They later told me that because I talked and acted so confident, they did not even consider I could be a student. Had they known, they would have told my instructor not to send me. Later, they also revealed the pilot in command (PIC) had hugged the right side of the runway with his plane to get traction that morning, as the middle of the runway was solid ice.

I got the plane out on the starting end of the runway, lining up in the middle as we had been taught, and began pushing in the throttle. I immediately started sliding left. This is not uncommon due to the torque effect from a piston single-engine propeller. It influences the movement and control of the aircraft. It is generally exhibited as a left-turning tendency. To counter this effect, a pilot is trained to put pressure on the right rudder to bring the aircraft back to the right or in this case, toward the middle of the runway. Well, I was warned about using the rudders when the runway is slick. As I increased the plane's speed, the plane increased veering left. I thought it would react like a car on ice, pick up a little speed and you can usually straighten it out. In the seconds it took from a slight veering left to realizing I was in deep shit, I slammed in the right rudder but hit the two-foot concrete-like berm at about fifty-five miles per hour. It felt like I hit a brick wall. If it had been loose snow on the edges of the runway, I would have just slid off into the fluffy snow and came to a stop. That would have ended my flight for the day, because I am sure I would have been pretty shook-up. But remember what is the belief, the story, I had played in my mind every day for a year? I would crash; it was just a matter of when.

By the time I slammed in the right rudder, it was too late. Sliding into the berm at over fifty miles per hour seemed liked it was happening in slow motion. The plane flipped up in the air, landing upside down on the hard-packed snow. The fuel tanks located in the wings were both full, and fuel was streaming out both sides. In the commotion, I forgot to turn off the magnetos, which ensure the engine continues to run in the event of alternator or battery failure. This meant the engine was not off, which could have ignited the fuel and had a catastrophic result. I was more concerned with getting out of the plane and that was difficult from an upside-down position. Those movie scenes of a crashed plane exploding in a ball of fire raced across my mind.

In all the lessons I had, we never practiced getting out of a plane upside down. It is a hard drop on your head when your seat belt is released. I unwound the cords from my headset and scrambled out of the plane, crying as I thought of the monetary damage and the flight-scheduling impact I had just caused. Running and almost falling on the ice, my instructor was yelling, "Are you okay? Are you okay?"

Me, screaming through my tears, "I'm sorry, I'm sorry!" I was okay, but the plane was not. It reminded me of a large piece of bent tinfoil, and in that moment I realized why so many small plane crashes end up tragically. I was lucky that my crash occurred while taking off and not while landing. My experienced pilot friends consoled me that I might have been severely injured or even killed had I hit the ice while landing. Likely I would have overreacted in using the rudders and/or brakes, they surmised. If I would have then hit some dry payment, the plane could have flipped, and a fire could have started. Those comments made me feel a little better.

The plane had to sit there until the National Transportation Safety Board (NTSB) and the Federal Aviation Administration (FAA) could do an investigation. As my instructor and I were retracing our preflight steps that morning, we discussed the pilot who radioed she was on downwind and then final for landing, but did not land. This happened before we fueled up the plane. She pulled up at the last minute and flew out of sight. Perhaps she saw something about the condition of the runway that made her uneasy. My instructor and I both thought it was odd, but not knowing her, we did not think too much about it. When the two pilots I was speaking with while fueling returned and saw the flipped plane on the side of the runway, they were stunned and wondered what had happened.

Because my head had hit the instrument panel on impact, I was getting a headache and stiff neck. I was still weak in the knees and felt a little sick to my stomach. I called my folks first thing. Mom answered, and

I tried to hold back my tears and quivering voice as I asked to talk with Dad. The minute he answered, I burst into tears and told him I crashed. Once he knew I was okay, it really did not seem to be a big deal to him. I was safe, and that was all that mattered to him. Accidents happen, right? But how much of this accident was caused by my strong belief of crashing? Luckily, I only hurt the plane and no one else. Do you think it was possible and maybe even probable that my thoughts, feelings and belief strongly influenced the crash? Had I created that manifestation?

After answering some questions over the phone with the NTSB, I drove home. That was a long two-plus hour drive, but I remember feeling a bit of relief that the accident was over. I knew there would be no more mishaps. I felt guilty wrecking the plane and impacting other student pilots. One of my dear friends, who became a pilot some months before me and was taking lessons like me, was now without a training plane. I felt awful.

There is some humor to this story. I love to find the humor whenever I can. That was a Sunday morning and the following Tuesday morning I had an early-morning meeting before going into the office. I was on the board of directors for our regional economic development corporation. I took my seat next to a long-time member who was also a pilot, I found out that morning. Before the meeting started he leaned over and asked, knowing I was a student pilot, "Did you hear about the plane that crashed up near the Canadian border?"

I tried to hide my shock and shame and sheepishly gulped, "Yes." He went on to say that he saw it on the news, and it was his plane that crashed. He had originally sold the plane to a small local public airport in Spokane, as a training plane, and they eventually sold it to the Fixed Base Operator (FBO) in north Idaho. Even though a photo of the plane made the news, my name was not released. I did not have the courage to divulge it was me who had crashed his plane. The meeting started, thank goodness. When it concluded, I high-tailed it out of there before he could say any more and possibly find out it was me.

I had never revealed I crashed that plane, until recently. I was giving a talk and using this example to demonstrate the power of our beliefs. Before the day of my speech, I researched the whereabouts of that board colleague who originally owned the plane and found out he died a year earlier. During that presentation was the first time I confessed to crashing a plane, his plane. It got a relief-filled laugh.

There was no way I would not have crashed. I focused on it a lot, so much so that I believed it to be true until it came to fruition. You may be wondering why I would even put a thought of crashing a plane in my mind, because it seems irrational. Why we do the things we do may remain a mystery to us and to those watching us. My belief became a self-fulfilling prophecy.

The other example is also about becoming a private pilot. Again, I used my thoughts, feelings and beliefs to manifest a positive outcome. When I started preparing for the oral and practical (checkride) exams, I visualized successfully passing both. The shower is a good place for me to think. The sound of the water is like white noise, and I am alone with my thoughts. The fact that the crash was out of the way, I needed to believe the rest would manifest positively. So, every morning in the shower, I visualized the examiner being pleased with my oral responses and nodding in approval throughout the checkride. In my mind I felt him shake my hand as he congratulated me on becoming a private pilot. I even visualized him signing my certificate as we stood at the counter inside the flight office and me signing it, as well. For the few months leading up to the big day, I consistently practiced those thoughts every morning.

But because I held the crash in my subconscious, the early stages of visualizing my successful checkride caused me some angst. The more I visualized perfectly performing each maneuver, however, the more confidence I developed. Extreme nervousness diminished to slightly being nervous to eventually feeling confident because in my mind, I had already performed perfectly.

That hot, sunny day the following August, I showed up confident. Guess what? It happened exactly like I had visualized and rehearsed it in my mind, including the examiner's handshake. He shook my hand as he congratulated me on my success and signed me off. He did this in the exact spot in the office I had visualized so many times before. Just like believing I would crash, I also strongly believed I would get my pilot's license. How could one person make two opposite things happen when neither was real, until I believed them into reality?

I hope you are thinking about your life and the things you have accomplished. The myriad of things you have done, and the fears and obstacles you have overcome. Think about why you accomplished some of them. Do you see any consistencies in terms of your thoughts, your feelings and your beliefs leading up to the success? Did you believe you would accomplish them? What about the things that have slipped through your fingers? Your desires, dreams and goals and those things that did not come to fruition. Could it have had something to do with your beliefs about those things?

I am passionate about sharing my experiences with others, because I keep proving to myself both positively and negatively what I believe. I often shake my head in amusement when something goes wrong. I no longer get frustrated but rather, I look back to see where I went off course. It always comes down to those same three things about what I have been focused upon. When I focus on a problem, I get more of it. When I focus on a solution, a solution appears. But I need to believe, really believe, and feel that the solution will come. I do not need to figure out how I will solve the problem. I just need to focus on what I want to happen and believe it is so and then be open to receive the answer.

Sharing my missteps may help someone else avoid something similar, and sharing what works just makes me happy. You may be where I was. In the beginning, I questioned the validity of positive aspirations and thoughts. Could it be that simple? Yes, it is that simple and/or that difficult, depending on your life's conditioning. The fact is true for all of us. It is our life, our choices.

Reading and listening to positive information reminds me that I like being in control and moving in the direction of my goals. I believe in lifelong learning, asking questions, talking with others and researching. I treasure positive quotes. I have two sets of *Law of Attraction* cards that have one quote or saying for each day. I have a thought-for-the day calendar, and I am reading multiple uplifting books.

Filling my heart, soul and mind with good thoughts makes me feel good. There is so much negativity in the world that sometimes it seems to override all the good. I am writing this during the COVID-19 pandemic. Our country, state, city and neighborhoods have been shut down or restricted for several months. The news is mostly about fearing the virus and how it has affected our health and our economic prosperity. I am not a fan of mainstream news, because I question the balance of the news being reported. There are always more negative stories than uplifting ones. I have some friends who say I am not facing reality and burying my head in the sand. My reply is I do see the reality; I choose to not put my focus on the negativity and all that is wrong, but rather look for solutions in the small, but important, silver lining.

I am not worried about contracting the virus, because I am not focused on it. I turn my thinking into believing I am well. When I find myself starting to worry, I remind myself of a saying that my sister, Jan, reminds me of when I am complaining or worrying out loud. She is my mirror and lovingly reflects, "Well, you just told me what you don't want. Now tell me what you do want." I love that about her. She helps to center me so I stop worrying something bad into my existence. Life is so interesting. Though we do not know the future, I like knowing I am shaping my future every day with my choices.

I tend to be much harder on myself than I am on others. When I am coaching or mentoring someone, I remind that person how perfect they are just as they are and the valuable role they play in shaping the outcome of their life. Yet, I seem to lose patience with myself and quickly criticize my mistakes or negative thoughts because I should know better. If we only treated ourselves as well as we treat others. What do you do on a daily basis that makes you who you are? Do you reflect on what you are reading, what you are listening to, with whom you are hanging around and who you are believing?

One of the first things I did to get a better handle on my thoughts was to tune into them throughout the day. They ran wild and free in my head; rarely did I check in. It was a little difficult at first. An entire day would go by, and I would not remember tuning into any feelings. I tend to get migraines, and the doctors had me focused on what I was eating and drinking, which is logical. What about my thoughts and beliefs? What about those quiet tapes running silently but impactfully in my mind without me realizing it? I really worked on getting more in tune with myself throughout the day to catch a new feeling as it occurred and to stop and think about what I was just thinking about. It was awkward until I consciously did it more consistently. I got better at catching the migraine at the onset and questioning what I was feeling and thinking that might be causing this physical reaction. If I realized I was feeling down, I would stop and question the reason behind that emotion. I do not believe any of us are completely happy with our lives every minute of every day. However, we can make more conscious choices about what we think, feel and ultimately believe.

My brother and I used to talk almost every morning when we were both driving to work. It usually took me about forty-five minutes from my house to the office. Tommy was driving eighteen-wheel rigs before he retired, so he usually had time to squeeze in a phone call. I enjoyed those talks with my older brother. He has always treated my sisters and me with love and understanding. He was always so supportive, as if he felt our hurts and our joys as much as we did. I leaned on his love and still do.

During those talks we would share how we were doing with being aware of our thoughts and feelings and what was playing out in our days. One thing he was kind of struggling with was inconsiderate drivers. If you can, imagine how tough it is to be a trucker in a large city like Seattle, Washington. Most drivers see truckers as in their way or slowing them down, and most drivers do not try to make truckers' driving any easier. He would get frustrated when another driver was inconsiderate or cut him off and he immediately felt his blood pressure rise. I could relate to the feeling and shared with him the game I would play. I told him I would make up a story about why the person was speeding or weaving in and out of traffic or cutting me off. Some of the stories I still use are: she's late for an interview or he just found out his wife is in the hospital and he is racing to get there, etc. I even say those made-up stories out loud in an understanding voice. As those motorists whiz past me, I wish them well and ask God and their guardian angels to safely get them to their destination. I always feel better when I do that and let the rant go. Tommy said he was going to try it. In those instances, I made a choice. I chose to create a new belief about their actions. I doubt those drivers were targeting me. It had nothing to do with me or making me mad or pissing me off. Those were emotions I reacted with, chose to feel, in the heat of the moment.

I believe almost everything is a choice. Some awful things can happen, but we still have a choice on how we react, what we think and feel and what we choose to believe. That brings the onus back on us, unfortunately or fortunately. I would rather be in control than let someone else have control over any part of me. I would rather be mad or sad, because it was my choice.

Because I choose to think positively when I wake up in the morning, I am usually energized and ready to take on the day. I believe it will be a good day and immediately start thinking about all I am grateful for. Gratitude permeates every part of my day. Before I get out of bed, I relish the warmth and comfort of my mattress and the coziness of my blankets. I breathe in the fresh air from the open slider door and from the small window high above my head. It smells like God, like nature, like wonder! I do not have to worry about what is out there. There is no fear of war or devastation. I can get in my car and drive to wherever I want and do whatever I want. Living in the United States is such a taken-for-granted blessing.

I leave the warmth of my bed and start my daily routine, which is feeding my cat, Sweetie. Before my dad passed away, he wanted one of us kids to take the semi-wild spayed cat that lived in his shed. Dad had a soft spot for all animals, as do I. Though I did not want a pet, I could not imagine her going to a stranger. It only took a second for me to respond, "I'll take care of her!"

She makes me grin each morning as she watches me take the canned food out of the fridge and put it in a small bowl. She meows in excitement as the microwave hums her favorite tune, breakfast! As I mix the food so it is evenly warm and not too hot, she excitedly talks to me. It is as if she is saying, "Hurry up! I've been waiting since your alarm went off." I delight in how she gets right in front of me and almost trips me up as we both walk toward my office where her water and food bowls are. She almost struts like, "I'll lead the way." I named her Sweetie because she is such a sweet kitty. As it is usually very early, I am usually in my robe. Because she is right in front of my feet, the bottom of my robe floats gently on her tail, my feet straddling her small narrow body, as we walk into the room. I am smiling the whole way. I put down the bowl, and she immediately devours the tasty morsels. I run my hand up her tail and leave her to eat. This morning ritual is so satisfying for me. I feel blessed for this little monster I inherited.

CHAPTER 13

ENDINGS ARE NEW BEGINNINGS

My retirement day was finally here. To my colleague's dismay, I wanted to leave with no fanfare. One of the linemen I worked with in my first big outage I managed said of his retirement, "There was no fanfare when I was hired, so I see no need for fanfare now that I'm leaving." That struck me as humble, authentic and egoless. He had done his job to the best of his ability and that was that. I hoped I had done the same.

I spent my last twelve years working in one of our company's outlying construction offices. One of the construction technicians asked what she could do for my last day at work. I told her I would love a maple old-fashioned cake donut from one of our favorite bakeries and a carton of milk. In my opinion there is nothing tastier nor more satisfying as cold two-percent milk with a freshly baked donut. When I arrived that morning, there was a hand-printed note on the desk in my office, "Do not come out until 9:30!"

Over those last twelve years, I often told stories of some of my antics as a leader during my career. I told the Nerf-gun fight story one morning to those construction technicians and field engineers. I, too, had been a field engineer, which some of them did not know, before I was promoted to the manager of that group.

As I wildly told this story, acting out some parts, the techs and field engineers listened intensely. By the looks on some of their faces, they seemed surprised by what they were hearing. I advised them that had anyone from the Glass Palace come in, like the president, I would have been in big trouble. For ten minutes of Nerf gun shooting, we were comrades in war, not work colleagues. We banded together and were fighting for an unknown cause and doing it with zeal and passion. What fun!

Apparently this one tech remembered that story. Unbeknownst to me, she told everyone in the construction office to bring their Nerf guns from home, many of which did not belong to their kids, but were prized weapons of the parents. She urged them to bring lots of ammo. Oh, did I mention the tech who left me the note also left me a very small Nerf gun with only four foam darts? I immediately knew what was up. She had remembered my story, and I was sure I was going to get it once I stepped out of my office.

I could hardly contain myself waiting until 9:30. When the time came, I discarded my high heels, because this was going to be war. I was known for scurrying around the office, walking swiftly and with a purpose. It was common to find me shoeless, because I could move around quicker than in my outfit-matching high-heeled shoes. I crouched down and snuck out of my office, peering around the corner…so far so good. I strategically positioned myself behind a large row of long cubicles, overhead storage bins and filing cabinets. I was stealthy and got off the first shot, then all hell broke loose! Every person in the office had a Nerf gun. Some were machine guns with rapid fire ammo. My paltry gun with only four darts, lasted about five seconds.

I ran around the office trying to duck shots but got pummeled with every step. I ran into one of the other boss's office to regroup. I then snuck behind an employee and used her as a personal shield. I grabbed an orange safety cone off the floor that was covering some cables and kept running, daring them to hit the cone, instead of me. One employee made a helmet from an empty cardboard box that contained spray cans to protect his face and add even more humor to the battle.

Out of breath, I finally surrendered. Laughing uncontrollably, sweating profusely and feeling the love this group had for this crazy lady was the best send-off I could have asked for. When we all finally put down our weapons, everyone partook of the donuts she had supplied for the whole office. I had my special maple old fashioned cake donut and my milk. Everyone stood there still laughing and chatting about the fun. I hope I conveyed my pure delight and thanks for the perfect retirement send-off. They could not have honored me in a better way.

They kept standing there, surrounding me as if waiting for a speech. So, after thanking them and especially thanking the organizer for remembering my story of a previous Nerf gun fight, I told them this is what work is supposed to be about. It is important to have fun, to celebrate the daily work they do which has extraordinary impacts on our customers. How they show up to work each day, has lasting effects on how they perform individually and as a team. It is important to feel and act like a team.

I urged them to support one another even when they get annoyed or pissed off. They need to instigate fun and not wait for the manager to do it. Laugh, live, and enjoy each day with each other because this day, today, will never come again. That last day of work was one of the most satisfying and delightful days of my thirty-nine-year career. For me it has always been the little things that make or break a moment. This little thing was really a big thing.

As I continue to find blessings disguised as challenges, I know that what I think, feel, believe and then act "as-if," makes up the daily interactions with family members, friends and work colleagues that turn out to be the life I am living. My belief that someone hindered my advancement—and my resentment about it—only affected me. I gave away my control and let the perceived negative thoughts, feelings and beliefs of another, become my own. Looking back, I am happy to have had the exact journey I did. Every instance and situation, failure and success, each disappointment and accomplishment, has made me who I am today and serves me moving forward.

What I continue to learn is there is no one holding me back, but rather I hold myself back and limit my growth potential by the choices I make. That happens when I am moving so fast that I cannot hear my inner voice. I let life's distractions disrupt my focus, and I am not aware of my thoughts and feelings. During those times in the past, I did not think to ask myself what I was doing to contribute to the outcome of what I was experiencing. It is okay to take some time to figure out where you got bumped off the path to well-being. And I recommend not spending a whole lot of time there, because by focusing on those past hurts and current annoyances and possible resentments, you just get more of the same. It is better to take your eyes off what is occurring in the now, if what you are seeing is not what you want. It is better to look where you want to be going and focus on the things you do want. This is similar to what I was taught when learning how to ride a motorcycle. Keep my eyes on where I want to go, not down on my bike, where I am.

The challenge for me is to notice when my thoughts are running amuck. It usually happens because I am not paying attention to them or not noticing a change in my feelings. I want to get out ahead of what is occurring, pre-pave what I want to happen next and get off cruise control and actively drive my life. Changing any habit that I want to change takes focused attention about what I desire and tuning into my feelings which are my trigger to stop and take notice.

Do you ever have something go wrong in the earlier part of your day? Have you ever thought, oh great, it is going to be that kind of day? Do you find yourself waiting for the other shoe to drop? I used to believe bad things happened to me in threes. Once those three things happened, I could get back to a more positive day. Does that sound familiar with, "I just need to get that plane crash out of the way and then everything will be fine?"

With my new, enlightened thinking, I wondered if I could change my rule-of-three belief. The next time I stubbed my toe on the bed frame as I was making the bed in the morning and the thought of *oh boy, here I go again,* I stopped. Rubbing my toe, I wondered if stubbing my toe was the Universe's way of getting my attention, slowing me down and forcing me to be present. There is nothing like stubbing your toe, especially your little toe, to get your attention!

One day I decided to choose better-feeling thoughts instead of my tried-and-true rule of three. I chose to appreciate the interruption and possibly the wake-up call. I then chose to make it a great rest of the day. I have not had a negative rule-of-three day since. You may be scoffing at this, but I urge you to try it before poking holes in it.

We all are on life's journey, and our journey is just that, ours. Our paths cross and intersect and sometimes get jumbled together at intersections. I hate it when I let my path, my thoughts, get mixed up with the paths and thoughts of others. When that happens, I need to refocus and get back on my path. It is really just as easy or difficult as that. It is awareness and choices.

Here is the simple three-step process I use to manifest what I want. Step one, I get in tune with my thoughts throughout every day. I proactively choose good-feeling thoughts. Step two, I recognize what I am feeling. If I want to feel differently, I choose different thoughts or start by thinking of past things that made me feel good. Step three, what are my beliefs? I choose beliefs that serve me, not swerve me. What I believe, IS!

My starting place is to let go of what is, if what is, is not what I want. Sometimes my dreams are so big that it is difficult to think positively about them. I initially may have feelings of doubt or fear, which results in a limiting belief. So, I turn my focus to thoughts that bring me joy, which makes me feel better and happier, which draws more of that into my life.

The more I focus on the positive, the joy and abundance in my life, the more similar thoughts and feelings I have and the stronger my positive beliefs become. I have had and will continue to have life influencers, those who believe in me and those who doubt, which brings me back to the beginning.

My thoughts, my feelings and my beliefs are always influencing the outcome of my life. What I am currently living is a result of prevalent beliefs. If this is new to you, start with a belief that is not deeply rooted. Finding something easier to start with, in terms of changing a belief, is a good place to start.

What do you want? Okay, ask. Believe God, Source, or the Universe has heard you and has already responded. It is yours for the asking. Have the belief your desire is granted, just waiting for you to let it in. First, be cognizant of your feelings. Your feelings, your emotions, are your indicator of your thoughts. Once you quickly examine your thoughts, your beliefs will become apparent.

Be in the moment. Feel the changes in your body during the day as your feelings shift in-and-out of good/not so good/good. Stop and ask, "What was I thinking to cause this feeling?" If you do not like the feeling, change your thought. If you like the feeling, keep feeling it and other good-feeling thoughts, and you will draw more of those feelings to you.

Choosing to get in tune with your thoughts, feelings and beliefs is like finding a soulmate connection. When you ponder why something has happened, remember my "a-ha" moment. A profound question revealed a life-altering answer to this simple question: "Do you mean to tell me that my belief the VP was holding me back was what was actually holding me back from reaching my goal?"

"Yes."

Your beliefs are the reasons why.

ABOUT THE AUTHOR

Patty! Shea is a relationship specialist savant. Her positive outlook on life and abundant supply of energy and enthusiasm come from a belief in what her mother repeatedly told her, "You make your own happiness and your own sadness."

For those who find themselves challenging the status quo or experiencing some self-doubt and resistance, her rich stories of quick-wit, not taking herself too seriously and her belief in possibilities, offer a framework for self-inquiry and exploration into the impact of your thoughts, feelings and beliefs.

Her forty-two-year career provides thought-provoking life lessons from a variety of industries. She holds a Master of Business Administration degree and is working toward a Ph.D. in Leadership Studies.

Patty offers guidance and solutions to individuals, groups and organizations to help people achieve greater self-awareness, self-esteem and personal growth in order to meet their life goals.

Visit Patty's website: https://PattyShea.com
Contact Patty at Patty@PattyShea.com
(509) 953-3986

If you enjoy this book, Patty would appreciate you posting a review on Amazon.

CPSIA information can be obtained
at www.ICGtesting.com
Printed in the USA
LVHW080059250722
724317LV00005B/26